Love your Haters

Compiled By

Angela Covany

HAVANA BOOK GROUP LLC.
HAVANABOOKGROUP.COM

HAVANA BOOK GROUP LLC
2173 SALK AVE, SUITE 250
CARLSBAD, CA. 92008

COPYRIGHT 2021 All rights reserved.
ISBN: 978-1-7353-1178-4

Table of Contents

INTRODUCTION

This unique Anthology is one of the most life-changing books designed to enlighten others by sharing the importance of self-love and forgiveness that has been created. Most people do not love their haters and simply reciprocate hate with hate.

LOVE YOUr haters was designed to help people realize that learning forgiveness towards them is a gift to yourself. Through the transformational process of learning how to forgive, you can release the negativity that is keeping you from living your best life.

This first volume of *LOVE YOUr haters* is filled with heartfelt stories from 25 different Authors sharing their stories of pain and triumph. Each story offers words of inspiration and healing.

All the Contributing Authors have shared personal stories of how replacing hate with forgiveness and self-love has transformed their lives.

Along the journey, life can get so overwhelming we can lose our identity in the process of putting other peoples' needs above our own. By practicing self-love and self-care we can become better versions of ourselves and create healthy relationships with others.

Solutions can be found throughout these pages. This book will be resourceful in many ways and serve as a positive attribute for your personal development journey. You will learn to love yourself completely and trust in the process that love always wins.

Kimberly Anderson

Forgiveness is taking your power back

by Kimberly Anderson

Love your haters...that is quite a statement. What does it mean exactly? I know when having conversations around that it oftentimes creates a visceral reaction. However, I know for me, when I break it down, it goes to loving myself. It is about how far I have come and the lessons I have learned over the years. When we go through something, for me it was domestic violence, it teaches us things we could've never learned about ourselves. Looking back, it is a reminder of how strong and courageous I am. How brave. Looking back, it gave me the understanding of where my power comes from.

For years, I always heard to forgive people. I didn't want to. I never had any intention of forgiving the people that have hurt me, my children or did those things. For me, I would never give them my forgiveness. How could I? Then, while I was going through my yoga teacher certification, I had finished an hour yoga practice, and sat down outside to meditate. I sat in silence, closed my eyes, and opened my mind to all that was around me. I started breathing slowly, deeply, allowing my mind to just shift into gratitude. I started thanking God for the light breeze that was blowing by me, for the birds chirping, for the warmth of the sun on my skin. I thanked God, for my children and their health and safety always. I sat there, thanking God for all the people and things in my life, for the blessings all around me. I thanked God for the abuse I had endured......In that moment, I jumped back, and yelled aloud, what the F*-k! and I started crying. I was shocked that that had come out of my mouth. Why would

I thank God for abuse? I sat there. Then, there was a peace that came over me, and I understood that without all that I had gone through, I wouldn't be who I was. I am uniquely me because of ALL of me, all the parts of me, all the things I have experienced, just like you. I understood in that moment, which going through all that I had, gave me the wisdom and deep understanding that I can now help others on levels I wouldn't have been able to otherwise. I know, I have been there, I remember, I know the feeling, I understand.

It was during that time, that I understood, that forgiveness wasn't for the abusers, or the people that hurt us. It is for us letting go of the hold they have over us. It is taking our power back. And that is what I did. It was slow at first, because I spent many years bitter and angry. It certainly wasn't going to happen overnight. As time went by, I started releasing more and more, until now, I feel nothing. There isn't hate, there isn't love, there isn't anger...just appreciation of who I am today, and how strong I know I am. I understand now that forgiving is really taking our power back. When we forgive, it truly sets us free from the hold, and when you allow that, you are no longer burdened by whatever trauma you have gone through.

When I share with people how to step into their power and speak their truth (which is my motto), we talk about beliefs, mindset, as well as forgiveness. I know now that all of those things are a part of who we are. We not only have to forgive the people that hurt us, but more importantly, forgive ourselves. We are deeply angry for winding up in those situations, or who we became during those situations, we start to not trust ourselves, I know I didn't. I couldn't believe I kept winding up in situations that were sucking the life out of me, and that I was living aren't enough, that we deserve the abuse. We no longer think that we are strong. We take on beliefs about ourselves that we lack in all ways. That is so not true. It finally occurred to me that when we look back on what we have gone through, they are incredible reminders of how strong, brave, courageous, and resilient we are. Because if we weren't, we wouldn't be standing here today. You wouldn't be reading this right now, and I wouldn't have written it. We are stronger and braver than we can ever imagine. We are MORE THAN ENOUGH! We wouldn't know this had we not gone through what we did. When I started to understand this more deeply, I began to feel proud of myself. Not only have I gone through that, not only am I a survivor, but I am a thriver, and I am powerful! I hope you feel the same too.

As I have been preparing for the next series of my Goddess platform that I created and coming up with content for the Goddess wellness retreat, I received a download from the Universe. I am always open to receiving insight that I can share out. A little background first, I had been having conversations about topics, such as this book, knowing I was going to write a chapter in it. Also, the conversations around my Goddess platform, which is all about sharing your story. And it came to me one day, that although people can change, not all people are meant to. Sit with that for a moment. Some people are meant for their whole life to be the abuser, to be the narcissist, to be the antagonist of your life story, and to many others. I know for me I sat with this download for a moment. That had never occurred to me. I had always wondered why the bad guy in my story always seemed like they got away with everything, and always leaving a trail of victims. Some people are not going to change, because their life path is to be the one that is testing us. They are the ones taking us down these roads of pain, so we can find our true self. Our power, and purpose. I found this realization to have a profound effect on me, and in my understanding of these "types" of people. Which also allows for greater and quicker forgiveness. Imagine for a moment, all the people that have gone through trauma, what they have done in their lives, what their purpose has turned into? Non-profits are born out of people going through something and there was a need. My platform was born out of me discovering the power in sharing our stories with each other. We heal on a deeper level every time we share our story, and for the people that get to hear our stories, we offer hope. A way out, collapsing time for them to get help out of their situations or healing from it. We create when we have gone through something. It creates something in us that causes us to grow, to expand, to create beautiful things in our lifetime.

We would never know ourselves like we do if we hadn't gone through what we had. It is a reminder of our strength, courage, and bravery.

Oftentimes, we go through many things. It's not a one and done life lesson. We go through so many things in our lives. The traumas and happenings are what help to mold us, create us, it becomes a part of our knowledge and brilliance, you cannot get that kind of education in a book. You cannot understand someone's deep sorrow or hurt like you now can had you not gone through what you had. Be grateful for who you are and why you are.

Twenty plus years in and out of domestic violence, I still deal with things tied to that with my children. It affects us, it teaches us, even while it hurts. I thought I couldn't possibly go through anymore, I used to joke at 25 years old, that I had the life experience of a 50-year-old. As I approached 40 years of age, I started speaking and getting involved as a domestic violence advocate, I created a speech called "God thinks I'm a badass", because I couldn't believe all that I had gone through up to that point, as I actually approach 50 years old, I look back, and think, wow, life is really a journey. It ebbs and flows, and to be honest, I couldn't imagine it any other way. I can't imagine who I would be had I not lived the life I have. I love me, and I love my life. I haven't always, but I understand now the journey. When my husband and I found out we were pregnant in our early 40's we were so excited. Then, we were hit with a miscarriage, I was shocked. I had four kids between age 20 through 30. It never crossed my mind that I could have a miscarriage, another, and then another. Finally, we got pregnant, and it stuck. I remember how excited we were. I remember how I felt, and the sheer love I was experiencing for our baby and my husband. I remember how excited I was to actually be experiencing a pregnancy in a relationship full of love, and passion. When I had been pregnant before, I hated my life, I was living with the abuser, I tried getting out all the time, I was miserable. However, this time it was going to be different, and I was excited for every moment of this journey. Then 3 months in, we found out that our baby was a boy, and he had a genetic condition. We were told he might not make it; he could die in utero, he could make it to birth and live only a few minutes, all these were different variables...We cried, I felt like I was carrying both life and death inside me. He passed at 8.5 months pregnant. I birthed him sleeping. It was one of the hardest things I have ever had to go through. All my dreams for this life with a new baby was gone, all my excitement for having a baby with a loving man beside me, gone. My baby was gone. There weren't enough things I could do to fill that loss in my life. And there it was again, forgiveness. See it's not always outside of us that needs to be forgiven. I had forgiven myself for past situations I got into. I had forgiven myself for not trusting and listening to my intuition, because it was always there leading me and guiding me, I just ignored it. I had forgiven myself for all of those things, but what about this situation? I learned that this was where I was getting to know myself even deeper. This was unconditional love on a new level. It was timeless and boundless; this was also asking this little soul that I never got to meet to forgive me. Forgive my body, I didn't even know. I just knew that I loved him. And someday, I will get to know the deeper lesson that it gave me. For now, I know to love myself and to give myself grace.

So, loving your haters doesn't mean to love them, it's loving you because without them you wouldn't know your strength, courage, or bravery. Forgiving them is releasing you from the hold of the happening over you. Forgiving yourself, because it was just a part of your journey so you can be the brilliant beautiful being you are, and I are meant to be. Knowing that it's not always outside of yourself that you have to love and forgive, it's you. Go within, go deep, and know you are the most perfect being as you are, God doesn't make mistakes. You are perfect!

Angeline Benjamin

My Reflection: The Art of Self-Love and the Practice of Forgiveness

by Angeline Benjamin

I was born and raised in a country called Indonesia. As the eldest of six children, being Chinese as my heritage, I was expected to set an example for all my siblings, including my two brothers. In the Chinese tradition, most parents would invest in the boys first rather than the girls when it came to education. My parents were the first generation in our family heritage to treat all children equally whether they were boys or girls. My mom was very adamant that girls were as important as boys. My dad supported my mom's philosophy. I was blessed to have parents who dared to break the tradition. We were taught to have the confidence that we were as intelligent as boys. My parents always told us that we were smart and that we could study in any field we wanted as long as we were willing to put the work into it.

Growing up, especially being the eldest, I knew my duty. Come to think of it now, I felt that it was a privilege to be a leader for my younger sisters and brothers. However, they did not necessarily listen to me all the time but most of the time. Even now, whenever we get together, I still practice my leadership skills with my siblings. Some may say that I am bossy. I simply say that I know what I want, and I let my siblings know this. Also, I learned along the way that they respect my decision because they know I love them, and I put them as a priority in my life.

A few years ago, I learned about the art of "self-love" What does self-love mean to you? To me, self-love means being kind to myself. Let's not get confused with self-indulgence or selfishness. I learned this as I grew up in the United States. There are so many benefits of self-love. I found these out along the way from learning from others and reading several books and in the last few years from interacting with virtual mentors via the internet. It helps me to develop a positive outlook on life. It helps me to understand that nobody is perfect. While growing up, I reached for perfection. So, it helps me to accept my own imperfections rather than to become a self-critic. I have to learn to let go of certain things that are not healthy for me. I am a work in progress. Once I accept my imperfections, it helps me to pursue my passions and goals. I have found a way to pursue my passions.

Another benefit I have gained when I practice self-love involves helping me to build healthier relationships. I learned that happiness comes from within. When we are not happy from the inside, nothing can make us happy. We need to feel content within ourselves; we do not need to seek external validation. Once we are content with ourselves, we will learn to build a healthy relationship. Self-love teaches us to forgive

ourselves, and in turn, we forgive others who have hurt us or have taken advantage of us. Self-love heals our inner wounds. It helps us forgive and move on instead of having so much hatred within. It really does not benefit our health to carry so much hatred for somebody else who hurt us. It does not mean we need to forget. We learn from our journey in life, and we move on. As we learn, hopefully we are not making the same mistakes over and over again.

I did not realize growing up that my parents taught me to practice self-love. Growing up, there was no internet, no google search. I learned from my parents, teachers, and friends. There were not specific words of "Self-Love" when I was growing up. But I know one thing---my parents always taught us to be mindful. Anything we do has consequences, either good or bad. They taught us to be mindful and willing to own our actions.

When I was a young child, I was not aware of the discrimination against the Chinese in Indonesia. I did not suffer from discrimination, mainly because my parents protected my siblings and me. Why is there discrimination against the Chinese descent? One of the reasons was that the leaders who governed Indonesia feared communism. On September 30, 1965, a group of Indonesian military personnel captured and murdered six powerful high-ranking generals. From what I was told it involved a group that supported the Indonesian Communist Party. In the month that followed, the Indonesian military slaughtered hundreds of thousands of people in Indonesia; all were communists or alleged communists.

Because we are of Chinese descent, my parents wanted to make sure we were not accused of being part of the Communist party supporters. We were sent to the best private Catholic school. We were not allowed to learn the Chinese language or speak the Chinese language. To further protect us and keep us from discrimination and from being accused of supporting the communist party, my dad went to the court system and provided a written declaration to the Indonesian government that we all were born in Indonesia. Our Chinese names were legally removed to show we were willing to remove our Chinese Identity. My name became Angeline Liestyawati Benjamin instead of Bong Mei Lie. My dad chose Benjamin as our last name because it was his baptismal name. Angeline was my baptismal name. Liestyawati is my Indonesian legal name, and Benjamin became my last name.

Although my parents went to a great extent to protect us, one thing we could not change was our appearance. Being a woman with a Chinese appearance, my parents knew they needed to send us abroad to be able to attend a good university. There was a common practice that to be able to receive any preferential treatment parents had to bribe or pay for protection. My dad was a wise man. He realized when you bribe or pay somebody for protection, it will not end well. My parents decided to send my younger sister and me to study in the U.S., so we would have an opportunity to have a great education. Why am I sharing this story? We all suffered growing up from disappointments, discriminations, and abusive relationships, etc.

As I grew older, I met so many wonderful friends, mentors, and coaches; I learned we must learn to practice "forgiveness" and move on. It does not mean we should forget and ignore what happened. We learn from it and move on. I learned not to keep our hatred inside us and poison us. Who will benefit from our hatred behavior? Not the people we hate or others who hurt us. In fact, most of them don't care. Therefore, we are the ones who will be the victims. I have learned now to let go of those feelings, and instead, I am grateful that I have good health. I have good friends and a wonderful husband who loves and accept me as I am. I have a loving family, and I love them all. I am proud of whom I have become. As a work in progress, I continuously will learn from my life journey and from others who inspire and empower me. I am blessed to have had such loving and devoted parents. Unfortunately, both my parents have passed away more than a decade ago. I still miss them.

My parents raised us with discipline yet in a loving way. As girls, we were raised to be independent. They set many examples which I did not appreciate until I was an adult. Although my parents protected us growing up after I reached the age of 18 years old.

(I was then considered to be an adult in my country.) They let my sister and me live in a foreign country without their supervision. Later, as I became their age, my parents shared with me very wise and valuable lessons I would like to share with all of you. They told me it was very difficult as parents to let go of their children. "You do your best and know how to raise your children the best you know how with what they have then. When your children become adults, you have to let them go and live their own life and learn from their own mistakes." As parents, they said they would always be there to support us emotionally. This was their philosophy as parents---raise children with unconditional love and discipline them with a great education as a tool to help them to grow up to become successful, happy adults. I treasure this lesson from them. Once we were adults, it was up to us children to live our lives our chosen way. They hoped all the parenting guidance with which they provided us would help us to become loving parents. They succeeded. Another important lesson my parents taught us is to believe in ourselves. My parents always told my siblings and me that because we were smart if we didn't get good grades in school, it was because we did not apply all the talents and capabilities God had given us. We needed to try harder and learn from our mistakes.

Because of the confidence our parents instilled in us growing up, I have always thought I could be anybody I wanted to be. The question is how badly did I want it? Was I willing to work to achieve my goals? I learned along the way that it is important to find somebody who believes in us (besides your parents and siblings) to support us in achieving our goals and dreams. We will make mistakes along the way; learn from them and move on! Life is too short to keep blaming others. To ask for help is not a sign of weakness, it is a sign of strength that we know our limitations, and we are confident enough to ask for help. We have self-worth. As I grew from a girl to becoming a woman in the United States, I learned being a wife or a mother was a choice I wanted to make.

As I turn seventy-one in a few months, I am very content with the life I have. I am very blessed to have had supportive and loving parents, siblings, a husband, and friends. I will not take this life for granted. That is why I make it my mission to empower, inspire, and educate others who need my support so they can have the fulfilling, productive, and abundant lives I now have. I keep reminding myself that life is full of hills and valleys. I need to focus on the hills and be grateful for the good health I have. If I don't like something, address it or do something to change it. If it is beyond my control, I must let it go! It is not easy, but I always remember I am still a work in progress.

Dr. Barbara Berg

The relief of seeing your haters as master teachers

by Dr. Barbara Berg

I remember taking a course in college called "Family Relations". During the first-class session, it became embarrassingly clear I had no experience of having truly loving family relationships in my family of origin. In fact, I had no idea where to begin with it all.

You see, the family I grew up in was full of overwhelmed individuals who were too afraid of "losing" somehow, to consider the idea we could all get our needs met appropriately at the same time. Everyone seemed afraid that if one person got what they needed, the others would "miss out" and they "wouldn't get". We were all filled with fear, competition, and a sense of lack.

In fact, the only possible "feeling of concern" for someone other than themselves I recalled at all experiencing, was my mother's interest in my brother Howie having his way all the time. She'd often say, "Just give him whatever he wants from you just to keep the 'peace'".

Looking back many years later, I realize he was such a handful, and my father was no help in dealing with him, as he was generally away and definitely not interested in Howie, that she felt she only had me to somewhat lean on. The fact that I was only 4 years older than Howie didn't seem to matter. I was the only other person who was home at the time, and my mother needed all the "help" she could get.

The fact was, my younger brother, Howie, had, right from the start of his life, what is known as "Early Onset Schizophrenia".

When my mother came home with him from the hospital, everyone seemed

to know "something was wrong with Howie," except my mother. Apparently, he was "playing to a different drum" right from the start, and there never seemed to be a moment of peace around the house. There was always some commotion going on. My mother seemed to charge me with the task of acting as if Howie was normal; and that was never going to happen.

What I did find to be positive in my young life, was going to Girl Scout Camp and getting close to my friends and their families. While these other families certainly had problems of their own, they never seemed to be anywhere near as bad as those in my own family. So over time, I came to find it was a whole lot easier and heck of a lot more "normal" and satisfying to be almost anywhere other than with my own family relations.

So, as I grew older and took my inner beliefs about relationships and family out to the world, when I got married or into relationships, I was certainly convinced that none would ever be perfect and somehow by the "Laws of Attraction" and the part(s) I played, that I would only be attracting these situations that were all unfair. For much of the time, I kept wondering, "What is a nice girl like me, doing in a situation like this?"

This scenario seemed to be especially true at certain times in my life. However, one time was different, in that "leaving the situation" wasn't the right thing to do. I really wanted to STAY with this man, and it worked out well.

Over time, I began to just focus on my own life, my own activities, and positive moments in my own life. I choose to focus on the best parts of the relationships I treasure, and the issues seemed to go away. I thought that would never happen! I am often told that "when the lesson is learned, the people or the issue will just seem to dissipate or just go away.

I'll tell you-It didn't all come at once. At one point, I started seeing a professional who specialized in dealing with what kind of energy you have inside and seem to be putting out to the world. She reminded me of some of the medical intuitives I have gone to in the past. However, this time, I started to understand how it wasn't just a matter of what seemed to be going on with the other parties involved, but I really understood what my inner, unconscious beliefs were, I was inclined to keep attracting that kind of energy from other people no matter how I tried to tell myself otherwise. (I believe my other mentors were trying to tell me the same thing, but I just wasn't ready to really hear them!)

Since then, as I mentioned, I came across yet another mentor, who knew a lot about energy; and she told me I still held a lot of fear in my heart, at times out of habit, and I needed to unload a lot to not attract such discord again. She gave me a book to read, and it has been my manual on life ever since. - It is entitled, "The Classic Trilogy" by Florence Scovel Shinn. In it, are "The Game of Life and How to Play It", "Your Word is Your Wand", and "The Secret Door to Success". As I began reading this book word for word, sometimes reading parts of it over and over, it became so clear to me on the inside- not just on the outside- how forgiveness both of oneself and of others is absolutely key to healing; and without it, no real change can ever happen.

I am so amazed how you can know in your head such phrases as "forgive others and your heart will be lightened" or "forgive yourself and your load will be lightened." (Those lines just came to me in that form right now as I'm writing); there are so many ways to say it. - But if you don't get it on a cellular level, you'll never really get what forgiveness can really do or even is.

Somehow, when I began reading this book, I got so many insights about forgiveness, that I have come to see how important it is in the area of loving yourself and others- everyday. I will probably read it several more times.

About the same time a mentor told me to read the above-mentioned book, I started to find myself saying the Ho'oponopono Prayer. It is an ancient Hawaiian practice for forgiveness and reconciliation that my other energy mentor told me about a few years ago, but I just recently took it seriously to heart. I had come to see that much of the time I have been angry at others, I was also angry at myself for "putting up with it all" and making my own mistakes at the same time. In fact, I realize that I had been so filled with anger from the get-go of my life, that half the time, I imagine I wasn't sure about whom or what I was even angry about!

I also came to see those forgiving others without forgiving myself didn't work and forgiving myself without forgiving others didn't work. And somehow, saying the Ho'oponopono prayer seems to cover all the bases in a very calming and peaceful way. So, whenever I think of the suffering, I have allowed myself to go through with my relationships in general, and my own responses to them, along with anything else that ever feels like it hurts from the inside, I just say over and over:

"I'm sorry, please forgive me, thank you, I love you."

I can tell you that I just feel more love and safety emotionally inside. When any thoughts come up around those who have not wished me well in the past, I have a great regard from them as "master teachers."

For I have learned a great deal about life. I send love in the direction of those whom I perceived had treated me unjustly and that leaves room for me to heal and send better energy in their direction than I have in the past, whether it's returned or not.

Reading in Florence Scovel Shinn's "The Classic Trilogy" how "No Man is your enemy, no man is your friend, every man is your teacher.", has helped me to see how much quicker we can all get past the pain when we see that in every moment we can learn something, if when we are upset with someone and we quickly get to, "What am I to learn here?", rather than just "How horrible this other person is! "Then we can get more quickly to the purpose of how and why this all happened in the first place.

And along with all of this, it occurs to me that we still haven't learned our lessons fully and what we came here to do, until we get to a place of feeling love- for ourselves and the others who have joined in with us to be a part of our dramas in letting go of feelings of lack, fear, and feeling abandoned- all along the way.

Just writing this now as I am coming to a close, I picture myself loving my family members and others, remembering those moments when we experienced positive feelings for ourselves and each other. I wish them all well now. I recognize that wishing others well is actually wishing myself the same for my greater good and peace of mind. And to take a quote from Florence Scovel Shinn, "What God has done for others He now does for me and more!"- And feels so much lighter on my heart and soul.

Elizabeth Mejia Celis

Gaining My Wings To Fly
A Metamorphosis From Pain to Freedom

by Elizabeth Mejia Celis

Earth is a school for the soul. Our souls have been anchored on earth to experience love and pain. Love thy neighbor and bless your enemies. As I navigate through life as a captain navigates a ship, I have dealt with major storms and shipwrecks that have left me empty. Empty of possessions, empty from the heart and yet my will to live burns strong. I still have hope. Sometimes we must start all over again from rock bottom and create something new. Our experiences are constantly changing. people come and go from our life but what I have come to discover is that the people that have caused us the most pain become our biggest teachers.

Living through life's journey, I have come to realize that the biggest lesson one must learn in life is to forgive — even the unforgivable. We are always taught to love and have compassion towards others. Jesus was our biggest teacher of unconditional love. He said love your neighbor as yourself. What did he mean by that? A neighbor can be anyone, such as a family member, a friend and even a stranger. Treat others as you would like others to treat you. It seems like it would be a simple thing to do, but when we have a very painful experience it's hard to love the person who has caused you so much pain and trauma.

As a child I experienced many challenges. I was bullied and made fun of for having too much hair. Hair on my arms, legs, upper lip and even an unibrow. They connected like a bridge between two eyes, maybe they were the bridge between two worlds. Today, I am now in a better place and I am able to laugh about it.

I was also on the heavy side — as in chunky. If kids and people wouldn't be so judgmental and critical of others, life would be so much easier. We must learn to forgive them too.

I see myself reflected in Frida Kahlo, the famous Mexican painter. She wasn't bullied for her looks, but life gave her other painful experiences. In my case, "betrayal" is one of the most painful experiences that requires forgiveness because I have endured several repetitive patterns that fall under this category.

How did I deal with all the bulling throughout my life you might ask? I learned to ignore and become invisible. That was my superpower. Now, as an adult my invisibility has turned into a block to success that I must continually work on. I became very conscious of my looks because of the constant criticism so I made it a point to practice self-love and acceptance daily.

I learned about healing crystals and how they can assist you with healing. Two of my favorite healing crystals are rose quartz and amethyst. Rose quartz is used to open the pathways for self-love — loving yourself unconditionally. Amethyst helps you relax and destress, and it also helps with anxiety and depression.

When it comes to relationships it doesn't always mean intimate partners. I have learned so much from friends and even other people that I see in different circumstances. I am an observer and that is how I learn. Sometimes you really must put yourself in someone else's shoes to really understand how others feel, what they see and how they feel. I see people as my mirror image. Regardless of whether I like how they are, they might sometimes reflect something or someone that I don't want to be. People always have an opinion about things and it's okay. It doesn't mean you have to agree with them. When it comes to people you will find a lot of competition, jealousy, and criticism. If you really want something in life, go for it and live your dreams. It's okay if you fail.

You get up, you pick up the pieces and you learn from your mistakes. The strength to keep going and never give up will always resurface at the right time if you believe in yourself, have faith and hope. People will always talk. Let them! Let their words fuel you to prove them wrong. Always remember this:

People are going to do what they're going to do and there's nothing you can do to stop them.

Now about hate... It's such a profound word, and it can open very negative emotions, sadness, old wounds, and even anger. Hatred is the embodiment of negative emotions. I see hating as the core of repressed emotions that stem from different traumatic experiences in someone's life.

These emotions are hidden or trapped in our memory cells stored in our subconscious mind and they unleash themselves throughout our lives in different ways. Negative emotions revolving around "hatred" can manifest through a myriad of actions, people, body language and even words, among other things. The presence of a particular person alone can trigger negative emotions.

By this I mean that someone can be triggered to do something evil to someone else because it was done to them. They might see someone who reminds them of someone who caused them pain. For instance, a man might be resentful towards women because he had issues with his own mother during his childhood and as a result his detached relationship with his own mother affected his future relationships women in general.

Sometimes, we meet someone and for whatever reason we don't feel in alignment with that person and we're not quite sure, "why?" There's just something about them that bugs us. So, instead of making an effort to get to know the person, we make assumptions and we ignore them. We let them know by either our words, body language or even the lack of attention thereof that we don't like them and we stay away from them by excluding them because we feel either intimidated, threatened or jealous.

When people don't agree with something that you're doing, or have some type of opinion that is opposite to yours, hate begins to arise and become more visible. Everyone is entitled to their own opinion, but don't let that stop you. In the end, the only one making any decisions on your behalf is yourself. You don't always have to agree with them, but accept any opinion as a different perspective. Thank the person for giving you a different view. In either case respect is very needed.

The word "hate" or "haters" can cause triggers. Take a deep look inside yourself as to why it brings out certain emotions. Is it because you don't agree with someone? Is it because you have a different perspective or opinion? Are you being judgmental or critical? Does it bother you to see other people happy or successful? Does it bring out a painful situation from your past?

This may be an opportunity to open past wounds that need to be brought out for healing. They need your attention or as some people might say, they need love and light to heal. Old wounds can become shadows that are very hidden at times and create blockages. When we bring them up to the light, meaning we identify and acknowledge them, this brings an opportunity to review and see things from a different perspective, which opens us up for healing.

With my own personal experiences, I have found that the number one reason why people hate or don't like me is because they can't control me. As a free spirit I like making my own decisions, and when I don't follow what others dictate or suggest they become very resentful. For example, if someone doesn't buy your products and services or follows you in social media, don't take it personally. People react because of what's going on in their lives. We cannot control the behavior of others. We are only responsible for ourselves.

When I was a teenager, I grew up watching soap operas with my family. I grew up very curious about love. Like all girls, I would see love as a fairy tale and because my upbringing was very traditional, we were taught marriage is forever. If you have a sexual relationship with a man, you must marry him or stay with him forever.

Women have been conditioned to believe that they must accept and condone the behavior of their partners, and that's why they've been so abused for so long. I met my first love as a teenager right before my fifteenth birthday. While practicing drill team at an after-school program with my peers, an African American boy came into our campus and approached me and my peers. We thought he was hiding something in his pocket and that he had a weapon. He started yelling and calling us names. I tried to ignore him, and he decided to take me hostage. I was terrified! Of all people, why me?! Everyone was afraid and they did absolutely nothing to stop him.

My attacker had me climbing a fence to an isolated place around campus. I didn't know what to do. I tried liberating myself but I couldn't. One of my friends saw her friend passing by in his car and she told him what was going on. He immediately grabbed his bat from the trunk of his car and started looking for me.

Luckily, he found me at one end of the school campus before my attacker had the chance to hurt me. It was a close call. When he saw my friend's friend coming to my rescue holding a bat in his hand, the attacker got scared and ran away. We reported the incident to the school campus police, and the guy was later found, arrested and charged with assault and battery. Later on my peers, my hero and myself had to go to court for trial. We discovered that he had a police record and had been in juvenile hall.

The court day was emotionally, mentally, and physically exhausting. It took all day to be called in for an interview. At the end of the day the attorney for the perpetrator came out and told us it was all over; the aggressor was going to do time in juvenal hall and we were free to leave. Everyone was exhausted from being there all day. I always found it odd that our attorney didn't come out to say anything before we left. Something was not quite right but we left anyway.

Months later while walking home by myself I saw the perpetrator again. I had the scare of my life! I pretended not to see him and kept walking. He must have been on drugs; I don't think he recognized me. I was terrified! I made it home safe, but I lived in fear to run into him again. I was very grateful to my hero. Eventually we started dating. He was three years older than me. I know that it doesn't seem like a huge age difference for a 15 and an 18-year-old to date, but I was still in high school while he was already out in the real world working, going out to clubs and so forth. As a minor I couldn't do that yet. We had a very tormented relationship. My hero became my worst nightmare.

He was a womanizer that constantly cheated on me and he was still too young for commitments. At seventeen I became pregnant, and the relationship worsened. I used to ask myself, "Why am I putting up with so much from this man?" Well, I was blindly in love and because he was the first man I was with, I needed to make it work. I thought my love and his daughter would make him change but that didn't happen. After two years of going back and forth, I said no more.

Instead, I decided to I focus on my studies. I graduated from high school, attended a community college and graduated with an associate degree in photography. I've made great new friends. Friends that turned into family.

One day I was invited to a party by one of my friends from college. She introduced me to her brother, and we just hit it off from day one. He was a little shy, but he drove a white mustang, that caught my eye. We connected right away like love at first sight. We dated and months later we were married and expecting a little bundle of joy. He was very happy. He wanted a family, and I wanted a father for my daughter. We had a nice little family, three kids together plus my oldest — life was good.

He was an amazing husband and father to our kids. Little did I know he was hiding dark secrets that once out in the open destroyed our family. He had committed a great offense that he had to pay for with prison. My life turned upside down once again. I had to make drastic changes to keep afloat. I had to move in with my parents and rent my house in order to not lose it. I lost so many things. I had to start from rock bottom again.

My heart wanted to help him. I forgave him, but I could not change what he did. It was very shameful. I wanted to hide under a rock and I avoided being around people so I wouldn't feel obligated to explain anything. I just didn't want anyone to know.

Men can do and say so much to women to the point it will turn their lives upside down. They have an innate ability to reel us in, and out of weakness we accept the degrading behavior because we want to feel loved. I was betrayed once again. I felt abandoned, unloved and unworthy, and my self-esteem had hit rock bottom.

Throughout our lives, at some point we can fall into vicious cycles or negative behavioral patterns that if left unattended, they act as heavy chains that are hard to break. I questioned God, why did I deserve to go through so much pain? Life can be so cruel! The pain was so unbearable I became ill.

I was not the kind of person that liked to cry in front of others. So, I would weep in silence. I would only talk to a few people, close friends and family. I had to be put on anti-depressants. I also developed stones in the gallbladder and an obstruction in my ducts. I underwent three surgeries to clear my disease. I almost died. I needed a lot of healing, emotionally, mentally and physically.

I had to learn to forgive even the unforgivable — not for them but for myself. Because I needed to live! I needed a life of peace without resentments. Hate is like poison, and it can do so much harm to your health. So, I chose to bless my enemies, but are they really my enemies?

As I reflect on my life, those people who caused me so much harm have been my biggest teachers. What did they teach me? They taught me about the power of compassion toward others, self-love, forgiveness and unconditional love, but most importantly they taught me about the value of self-respect and establishing barriers. They also taught me about the power of standing up for myself and not allowing others to disrespect me. By keeping this power close to my heart, I am able to make the right choices for myself and establish healthy boundaries. Within this power lies a sense of peace.

Breaking these toxic patterns is not easy. You really must work on yourself, but life is all about our experiences. As painful as they may seem, I am grateful for my greatest teachers. Thanks to them I gained my wings to fly! I am very grateful for the people in my life who were there to listen without judgement and comforted me, as well as my mentors and healers who have assisted me along my journey.

Self-care is a must as part of my healing journey. I love being surrounded by nature and grounding myself by putting my feet on the ground and touching the ocean water or rivers. Mother earth nurtures me and takes away my stress. Meditation is also a great tool. It quiets the mind to help you relax and function better.

During the pandemic, I also gained two more hobbies. I enjoy painting and creating gemstone jewelry pieces, which are also used for healing. Music is in my soul. I love to listen to music and dance to the rhythm of the beat. When I am out in nature, I love taking pictures of flowers, animals and the sceneries all around me. One day I will travel the world. There is so much beauty to see in this world, so many people to meet, and different cultures to learn from.

Thank you for reading my story. I hope it inspires you to look at life from another perspective. As a photographer for more than 20 years, I have learned that there needs to be darkness in order to see the light. Life is all about balance. The better equipped you are to learn how to create balance, the better your life will be. I balance different professions, the artist as a photographer and the protector as an insurance agent. It's not an easy task, but when you have the heart of service anything is possible. As a photographer this is my advice to you.

If your life doesn't turn out the way you want it, readjust your focus and take another shot!

Angela Covany

No Such Thing As A Perfect Person

by Angela Covany

There has never been a better time than right now, to realize we are all just perfect works in progress. Allowing empathy and gratitude to guide you will truly help you on any healing journey of transformation. A positive mindset will also help you see that the only way over pain is through it. Silver lining and happiness are found in the moments, just like sadness and despair are simply moments. I always like to think that what is happening right now is happening for me rather than to me. This allows a greater level of introspection. It is important to release limiting belief patterns and change the script of your life from time to time. After all, life is an ongoing process of change and growth. It is always good to get a broader view of clarity and perceptions.

Oxford English Dictionary Definitions.

FORGIVENESS: Root word is - Forgive-1. Past, part. 2. Stop feeling angry towards or about.

ACCEPTANCE: Root word is - Accept-1. Say yes to. 2. Take as true. 3. Resign yourself to.

There are ways to let go and find inner peace

Invisible vs. Visible, if you have something you can physically hold eventually, you find somewhere to set it down and get rid of it when you get tired of carrying it. You will put it down even faster if it is very heavy. Why is it so difficult to drop all the emotional weight? It is because even if we want to, we just don't know how and/or we do not possess the tools to use when we are triggered. Below are just a few things that I have found to be helpful. Please seek out other books, resources, and mentors to help you through this journey of seeking peace and embracing your self-love.

Gratitude

I live my life with a continual attitude of gratitude; I was raised that way. A lot of people may not have been. I wake up grateful for a new day. I look for gratitude in all things. I am grateful for all that I have every day, I am grateful for everything, I am grateful for the experiences, I grow from them all. I am grateful for the blessings I receive, the children I get to enjoy this life with, the people that I love, I am grateful for the people I meet and the very air I breathe.

God's Mailbox

There are times in life that I have not known where to direct things I wanted to say to people. I thought either they did not care to hear what I had to say, what my feelings were or simply would meet me with negativity. Sometimes those that I have wanted to have resolution within the past were not ready for resolution. We all have those people and situations. For this, I use God's mailbox. I write out a letter to whomever to release circulating thoughts and frustrations. To get it out of my head and heart to release it. I seal the letter in an envelope. I then keep it and can decide if at some point, it would be beneficial to send. I am not sure if I ever will, but for the time being, I just don't want to think about the situation any longer. This helps me to forgive, move on and release my thoughts. I have found it extremely helpful.

Anger in the Fire

This is along the same concept as the above but this one seems to work better for issues that concern anger or those you want to speak with and cannot speak with at all, even if you wanted to. The only difference is that the sealed letter is burned. I have very seldomly used this method because I have not carried a lot of anger for a while now. I have learned different, quicker ways to let go and forgive quickly. I do know others who find this method to be immensely helpful and therapeutic. I have been told that watching the letter burn helps anger dissipate. This has helped them in a psychological way towards their healing through traumatic past events.

Problems and Burdens

Often there are situations that have been so difficult that I thought, I simply could not bear the burdens in the moment. It was just too much to handle. I thought, please just take this and sort it out. In those specific times I have given these burdens to God, then I could focus on things I could understand and feel I could manage. With this method, I visualized the person or situation that is hard to feel or understand and imagine I'm holding it in one hand. I raise my hand upward and think ... here you go; I don't need this circulating in my mind, or I no longer want to feel this. I trust in God's perfect divine timing and infinite grace. I do not stress much, as I think this has been one of the best tools in my toolbox. It is so easy to do. I continue to use this method whenever I need to. If you do not feel comfortable with the concept of God or your understanding of God, you can hand it to the universe or the great abyss. You will still benefit from this method either way.

Empathy

Empathy and understanding are important! Why? They are pillars of forgiveness and love. Having understanding doesn't mean you can fix someone, nor does it mean you should ignore behaviors. To have empathy and understanding for someone also doesn't mean that others are pardoned for their words or actions to you. It simply helps you, to not take things personally and gives you clarity into whether you should continue to invest into a situation or relationship that doesn't serve your highest good. Choices are what determines your quality of life, your future, and your self-esteem to an extent.

How To Forgive Yourself

I do not live my life with much regret. I typically say, "I live with no regret," but I have made some poor decisions that I have had to forgive myself for making. Most decisions we make at the time we made them seemed to have good reasons. It's not until we look back in hindsight sometimes that we see that there could have been a better choice. We cannot continually beat ourselves up over past decisions or choices. We must forgive those past instances. Learn from them, do not repeat them and let them go. Always remember we are human. It is essential in forgiving yourself in life. We were designed to be imperfect. Not one person living on the planet, live without a regret or poor decision. Should everyone on the planet live mad at themselves daily? Of course not. Yet too many people continually struggle with their imperfections. The solution is forgiving yourself for expecting perfection from yourself. We are all on a learning journey of lessons, blessings, and seasons. We grow in maturity levels and spiritual levels as well. How humble could we be if we were perfect already?

When deciding that you want to know how to forgive others or yourself, I think the most important thing to realize is that you must have patience. In time, you will learn how to let go of the past, to feel the peace and to stop feeling the pain. Release what is or was out of your control. I am a firm believer that Prayer works best for this.

How to Forgive Others

Have patience with the process. Healing is not linear and what works for some may not work for others. Continue to try different approaches. Seek out specific mentors, therapists, or council. One of my favorite mentors for over 20 years is Louise Hay. I have learned so much from her wisdom. I recently saw a book entitled "I Can Do It: How to Use Affirmations to Change Your Life." Her audio version is available on YouTube. There is a tremendous amount of enlightening insight regarding forgiveness about 20 minutes into the audio version. I encourage you to read more books and attend support groups. You are never alone. Others can share with you what has helped them and perhaps, what they have done will work for you. Keep searching. When you have reached a place of healing through your journey to find forgiveness you will feel it, like a weight has been lifted. A feeling of peace. At some point in my life, I have experienced each of the types of abuse on the wheel of power and control. Most people who know me, know that it is not obvious to them because I have sought to educate myself. I have searched out to find out how to do the inner work and to continue with a forward mindset. You must go through to go forward. The other thing to think of is, who it is you need to forgive? We all have to realize there is no perfect parent, relative, sibling, child, boss, co-worker, teacher, etc. The fact that we had expectations with them is where we must also realize our own human expectations are imperfect and meet others with empathy and compassion for being human and faulted. (Everyone wants to believe in the perfect family dynamic, the perfect mate, or the perfect best friend. We were raised on fairy tale mentality). However, Abuse is always wrong. It is important to realize their actions or words were not deserved. In those instances, I guarantee you they were not. Most times inner negativity is outwardly projected onto others. Forgiveness is a gift for you, not for them. Chances are they were not even affected by what they did or said to you. In fact, I do not believe when people hurt you, they even know why. Hurt people hurt people! Not all people are designed with fair logic, good reasoning or have the capacity to show it. I think people also can only love you in the capacity they know how to or can learn to. Forgiveness is not forgetting. Forgiveness is the art of releasing the emotional and psychological negativity that no longer needs to keep you stuck, hold you back in your spirit, or future progress. Forgiveness can allow for the possibility after healing to have better relations. Even with those people you once couldn't see ever being able to forgive in the future, to be part of your present in civil and caring ways. Sometimes when others are willing to put the time and effort into doing the needed inner work for their own growth, wonderful changes can take place.

How to Begin to Truly Love Yourself

I think one of the most important lessons I realized when I learned what the journey and transformation of self-love looked like, truly came from a place of realizing I did not need external approval to love and embrace what was already designed perfectly imperfect. I remember thinking at one point, after trying continuously to be enough and better, that I was already enough. You can be more than enough for those who can't appreciate you for you. Perhaps they like other qualities in people and that is perfectly alright, it just means you should move on. You can appreciate what is and was and go forward. I didn't need to meet anyone's expectations and neither do you. I know who I am, and that others' opinions don't mean much if they are negative. Everyone has opinions. With self-love it is also important for you to set healthy boundaries for yourself. Surround yourself with those that appreciate you for you and will recognize and remind you of how much light you shine. What simply means more than anything else, is the opinion you have of yourself. Love yourself completely. There is a process of letting go of all the negative mind chatter that can tell you otherwise as well, but through many available resources and methods, it can be quieted and resolved. The process is much like rewiring hard wiring or reprogramming what was programmed by others. Do you know that you are already exactly perfectly designed in this life? When I think of how so many people say," this life sucks," and I remind them just how perfect it truly is, perceptions change. How far away is the sun and moon? Yet, you have the perfect warmth during the day and the perfect amount of light at night. We are no different. We are in perfect alignment with those who we will help and those that will help us to grow on this journey. Love yourself enough to know you are amazing, abundance is your birth right and you are deserving of all good things.

Verlaine Crawford

Three Keys To Healing Your Heart And Mind

by Verlaine Crawford

UNDERSTANDING, FORGIVENESS, AND LETTING GO

Many of us are overwhelmed by the continuous, stressful challenges we face in today's world. At the same time, upsetting memories of past experiences that hurt us emotionally, mentally, or physically continue to haunt us. Those traumatic events often leave deep scars that can hinder our relationships with other people, limit our communication ability, and stifle our progress professionally. We begin to see the world as a dark and dangerous place.

HOW DO WE HEAL PAST WOUNDS THAT LIMIT OUR LIVES?

We can talk about our upset and pain with a therapist to heal. We can attend workshops and read self-help books, leading us toward a better understanding. Yet, I have found that the "cure" to regain balance, a sense of safety, and self-empowerment is to understand what happened and forgive the people involved, especially ourselves. We need to release and let go of the injury, pain, and confusion in our minds and hearts.

IS UNDERSTANDING AND FORGIVENESS POSSIBLE?

At the age of 27, in April of 1971, I became Chief Copywriter for Jack Lawlor Advertising in the Equitable Life Assurance Building on Miracle Mile in Los Angeles. The months went by happily as I worked with a great team and Creative Director who imagined the visuals for ads, and I created the headlines and copy. It was exciting for me to work on many national accounts.

All went well until a sunny day in August of 1971. I left the office on the 15th floor at 5:30 pm and rode the elevator down to the parking garage, four floors under the building. I walked into a small room with two elevators facing each other and two doors at either end of the room. I turned left and walked toward the door closest to my parked car.

The door opened, and a black man dressed in a guard's cap and uniform walked past me. I looked into his eyes, and a voice in my head said, "Run."

I argued with myself, "Why should I run? I'm tired. It's late. Why should I run?"

Before I could reach the door, the "guard" had his arm around my neck and a knife at my throat.

My first thought was, "Oh, that's why I was supposed to run."

The "guard" with the knife at my throat started pushing me across the room to the opposite door. I could barely breathe with his arm tight against my throat. I tried to loosen his arm with one hand without disturbing the knife, and then I said the all-time great statement: "Calm down, you're hurting me." (Duh!)

At that moment, the other elevator bell rang. The guard transferred the knife from my throat to my back. The elevator door opened, and two men started to come toward us. I felt a thump in my back when he stabbed me under my right shoulder blade. The men pulled me into the elevator.

And then my lung collapsed. I slumped to the floor, thinking I was dying. The pain was unbelievable. A sentence came into my mind: "Dear God, if I should live, Make me an instrument of your

Peace." (I didn't know St. Francis of Assisi spoke that phrase.)

My rescuers rode the elevator with me to the lobby to wait for the ambulance. A wonderful young man who said he had served in Vietnam held me as I leaned against the edge of a table. The police filed past me, asking questions.

(The two men who rescued me were lawyers. One told me later that they had been in the elevator to go back up to the office, but he had a strong idea that they should go down to the garage to get their uniforms to play baseball later. He told me he felt like something was pushing him across the lobby to the elevator going down. (Thank you, Guardian Angel!)

The emergency room experience was also quite terrible as the nurse had great difficulty inserting an IV. At one point, I asked her to hold my hand. I wanted to feel like a human rather than a pincushion. Then the doctor came and stabbed me in the chest to insert a tube for my lung to reflate. I was in shock. My world had turned upside down.

When I was recuperating in the hospital, the agency owner's son David visited me. I was lying flat and could barely see him across the room. But I heard his words, "You know you'll have to forgive him."

"What?" I couldn't believe my ears.

"You'll have to forgive him," he repeated.

I said nothing. But David's words continued to echo through my mind in the years ahead.

LOOKING FOR THE ASSAILANT

After healing my collapsed lung, I tried unsuccessfully to help the police find my assailant for many months. The police said I was lucky.

"How was I lucky? I asked.

They explained that there were five other stabbings in that area (the Rampart Division of Los Angeles) on that same day. I was the only one who survived. That news was very upsetting.

I continued to try to go to work and never parked under the building, nor did I ride in the elevators alone.

One day the police called and said that the assailant might be in the lobby of the building. I asked if the police would be there. They said no.

"What if he tries to attack me again?"

The policeman answered, "Oh, they do that sometimes."

I gathered a few of my co-workers, and they walked with me into the spacious lobby. I saw someone who looked like the assailant about fifty feet away. I told the police, and they checked him out. He wasn't the one.

The uncertainty and fear continued for eight more months until March of 1972. It was Columbus Day, and the police came into our office and told everyone to vacate the building. There was a bomb threat on the 15th floor...our floor.

That was the final straw. I left L.A. and moved home to Carmel to heal from the experience of living in total fear. I went to a psychologist for three years, but I was still paranoid and living in fear.

INTEGRATING FOR WHOLENESS

A turning point in my life happened in 1977 when I attended a "Neurolinguistics Programming (NLP) workshop in Carmel. One afternoon, the leader (Greg) did an integration process that opened the door to healing the deep psychological wound that had kept me in constant fear for six years.

I told Greg and the audience about the stabbing. He asked my permission to take me through an integration. I said, "yes." He asked me to imagine the two parts of my being who participated in that event. (The following is my version of the integration technique that I call the Wholeness Process.)

Greg said, "Choose a hand to represent one part of you who believes the stabbing was a terrible experience and should not have happened. I chose my right hand.

"Now, your other hand will represent the part of you who thinks the stabbing did something _for_ you.

I winced at that idea. What did Greg mean, "It did something _for_ me?"

Greg: "Now I will ask the part who thinks it would have been better not to be stabbed: "What would have been the advantages of not being attacked and stabbed that day?"

I looked at him as if he were crazy. I thought for a few minutes and said: "Well, I would have been healthy physically and emotionally without that event. I would have stayed on my job, and I would feel safe in garages and elevators. I would be more at ease and sleep better."

"That makes sense," he responded.

"Now tell me the _advantages_ of being stabbed."

"Are you kidding?' I asked.

"No, get into the perspective of that part of you that thinks the stabbing did something _for_ you."

I sat and thought about what the advantages could be.

Finally, I said, "Well, my boyfriend, John, had gotten a job and an apartment in San Francisco. I was still living in L.A., and he returned to be with me."

I see," said Greg. "What else was an advantage?"

"I decided to move back to Carmel, where I could experience a more peaceful life. John joined me and I became Director of Sales at the Lodge at Pebble Beach. None of that would have happened."

"So, the stabbing put you on a new trajectory," remarked Gregg. "What else?"

"Well, my awareness increased. I now pay more attention to the world around me. I listen to my intuition and am gaining trust to follow my guidance immediately."

"I see," said Greg. "So even though you would prefer not to have had that terrible experience, you can see there were some advantages."

"Yes," I replied reluctantly.

"So, what if you could make changes and follow your intuition's guidance and you do not need to experience traumatic incidents in your life."

I became quiet and felt the answer: "That would be wonderful."

"Okay. Please close your eyes and keep your hands apart. We would like the part of you who thought this event would do something _for_ you to go to the Creative part of your being. Imagine a beautiful room filled with golden light. In the room are Angels that provide all the answers in the Universe."

Greg continued, "We are asking now for three ways you can trust your inner guidance so you can make changes easily and gracefully. You do not need to know what those three ways are in consciousness. You will simply act and feel differently."

He asked me to bring my hands together, intertwining fingers and moving my hands up to my heart. He suggested that I imagine all parts forming a huddle around the two in the center, and that my higher self now send love and healing to all parts of my being.

Then he told me to imagine the two parts of me walking up a grassy hillside and sitting on a bench overlooking flowers and a lovely stream. The two of them discuss how they will work together to heal and make me stronger. As a result of the integration, I had a new understanding. My energy became clearer.

I KNEW I HAD TO FORGIVE

A few years later, I knew I had to go that extra step and forgive my assailant and also to forgive myself for not listening to guidance. I asked my minister, friends, and family _how_ to forgive. But no one could give me an answer. And so, I asked God to forgive _for_ me and to help me let go of the event in my mind and heart. I cried tears of relief as I handed the responsibility of forgiveness over to God.

As the days went by, I felt the dark clouds over my head, the constant chatter in my mind, and the weight on my shoulders begin to lift and float away. I could see clear skies again. After a few weeks I felt at peace. I could travel alone, feel safe, and be free.

Do I love the man who stabbed me? I would say that I love the God Force that created him. I do not hate him, but I certainly wish that he could be imprisoned so he wouldn't hurt anyone else. Forgiveness helped me to release the perpetrator from my mind so I could move forward.

Since then, I have enjoyed a fascinating marketing career and have written four books. In the 1990s, I was honored to be invited to the Far East and Europe to guide people through personal growth workshops and private sessions. It is a great life, and I love helping people to experience the power of wholeness.

Contact Verlaine for personal and business consulting at

949-422-7602

VerlaineCrawford@gmail.com

www.CreativeLifeAdventures.com

www.VerlaineCrawford.com

Virginia Earl

The Scent of Burnt Almonds

by Virginia Earl

There is no love without forgiveness,
and there is no forgiveness without love.

— Bryant H. McGill —

This is one of the pieces of my life when the dial of space and time shifted 360 degrees. It was a moment in my life that took me years to heal, and till this day I have remnants of the trauma that occasionally follow me everywhere I go like a ghost from the past.

Over the years I learned to accept the image of the worst night of my life that is permanently stored in my subconscious mind as a warning. It's an emotional warning that's triggered whenever it deems it's necessary. It was a harsh lesson and one that I don't wish upon anyone.

Strangely, the sequence of events that gradually lead me into the horror of what happened on a cold winter night when I was dragged into what felt like a sinkhole of death, didn't come alone. It was accompanied by "the scent of burnt almonds," a bitter fusion of regular and sweet almonds that contains lethal chemicals and its byproduct is cyanide — the taste of death.

There have been other times in my life when I have smelled distinct scents in strange places, like the smell of roses at a library when my grandmother passed away but this one was different — it was frightful.

The white coat

After having lived in New York City for a while and getting mugged in broad daylight, I decided it was time for me to leave. I had enough! From one day to the next, I took a bus to Maryland and lived with some friends for a while in Silver Springs. Then, after a few months I moved to Arlington, Virginia, where I rented a room at another friend's house. She was like a mother to me, and she enjoyed having someone else in the house to keep her company.

It was January, the coldest month in the Washington metropolitan area, and it was snowing heavily. I didn't have the right coat to keep me warm, so I decided to go shopping. I went to different stores and tried on coat after coat, and nothing fit me. Finally, after hours I found the perfect one. It was a long, white down coat with a hood and it fit perfectly. I have long arms and I always have trouble finding coats, jackets, and shirts with the right sleeve length so when I tried this one on and it actually fit me, I was very happy. However, once I looked at the price tag, my heart sunk, and my excitement level vanished in an instant. As easy as it came, it left!

Although at that time I was working at an insurance company in Washington, D.C., funds were tight after the move from New York. I really needed the coat to keep me warm as I didn't have a car and I was dependent on buses and the Metro system to get around. Winters in the Washington metropolitan area are harsh. I had to have that white coat no matter what!

I called my sister in Los Angeles and asked her to help me. She thought the price tag was too high and wanted me to look for another coat, but for some strange reason I became obsessed with this white coat. I told her in between tears that it had to be this coat. I was adamant with my reply! I remember she kept asking me, "Why does it have to be this white coat?" I explained to her that I tried several other coats and that this was the only one that fit me, but it was also the color that made me feel it was the right coat. It was white, one of my favorite colors and my mother's favorite color. I did buy it and I was happy that I had a thick down coat that would keep me warm throughout the winter.

The walk across Key Bridge

It was a Friday night and after work I decided to go to Georgetown for a bite to eat. Back then Uber and Lyft didn't exist yet. Cabs were still a good choice, so I took a cab from work to M street in Georgetown. I had dinner at a restaurant that was located halfway down M Street and not far away from Key Bridge.

By the time I arrived at the restaurant, it was dusk and cold, but I felt I would be fine with my new, warm, and fluffy white down coat. When I finished dinner, it was already dark outside. I decided to walk to Key Bridge to save money on the cab fare, and then walk across from the Georgetown side of the bridge to the Arlington side and from there I planned to take a cab. I had a feeling that I probably shouldn't cross Key Bridge late at night, but I did it anyway. I tried to be positive and talk myself out of feeling fearful. I am five feet, eleven inches tall, and my thick and fluffy white down coat made me look even bigger. So, what could possibly happen? Right?

As I got closer to Key Bridge, I noticed that to the left of the pedestrian walkway entrance there were some trees and some people hanging out on the sidewalk, but I didn't pay much attention to them. There was a male wearing a baseball cap pacing back and forth. It was pitch dark as there weren't any streetlights at that end of the bridge so I couldn't see his face. Out of nowhere he said, "Hi." I didn't pay attention to him. All I cared about was getting home so I just kept walking as fast as I could down the pedestrian walkway on the left side of the bridge.

I sensed someone was walking behind me, but I was too afraid to turn around to see who it was. When I reached the end of the walkway in the Arlington side of the bridge, a man grabbed me by my waist and forcefully pushed and dragged me into the bushes to the left of the bridge. Within seconds time stood still — time froze all around me. It was as if I fell into a time warp and all of a sudden time and space were distorted and shifted everything into this deep, dark bottomless sinkhole.

Falling into the abyss

I was laying on my back while he was hovering over my body and holding me down at the same time. His head was facing the street so he could see anything and anyone who passed by. I realized then that it was the same guy who was wearing the baseball cap and pacing back and forth on the sidewalk by the bridge entrance. I was terrified! I couldn't move! I couldn't break away! My ability to kick into a fight or flight mode simply froze. He had me pinned down onto the ground.

Suddenly, I saw a black circle surrounding my body and his. We were suspended in time and darkness was all around us. It was as if in that space we had left this Three-Dimensional World and we were falling into the abyss.

The black circle that surrounded us within that time warp had a spiritual significance. Eventually, I came to the realization that the black circle represented the ending of a cycle and the beginning of a new one. It was an empty space in time, hence the time warp, which was waiting to be filled with either something positive or negative.

In one way, the black circle symbolized a positive transformation that was waiting for the right moment to surface, but on the other hand it also represented a symbol of grief, pain and challenges associated with letting go of emotional and physical attachments, not only for myself but for my attacker as well. It felt like we were being sucked into a dark, bottomless sinkhole. Within this time warp there were lessons that we both needed to learn and either we were both going to crawl out of it together, or one of us was going to die in it.

I couldn't hear anything outside of the circle, other than my voice pleading with all my might for my life, "Please don't hurt me! Please don't hurt me!" He said, "Shut up!" and again he repeated, "Shut up and don't move!" He was enraged!

Everything around me was blocked except for his body hovering over mine. In that time and space, I saw my life flashing before my eyes and all I could think of was my family, especially my dad, and what would happen once I was gone. My mum had already passed away when I was 17 years old and ever since her passing, my life had been one challenge after another, but this was a bit much...

If I must die...

As I laid there on the ground, while the sound of my heartbeat gradually got louder and louder, I continued to plead for my life while I swallowed my tears in a state of raging despair. I was in shock! My body was shaking. I felt my face flush — burning with rage. A feeling of anger, despair and helplessness increasingly took over my body.

At this point, I was afraid to move, speak and even breathe. I couldn't bare looking at his face so as my breathing got deeper and deeper, I closed my eyes. I felt that was the safest thing for me to do. While my eyes were closed, I kept breathing knowing that at any moment I might not hear the sound of my next breath — each breath that I took could be the last one. Listening to the sound of each breath meant that as long as I was breathing, I was still alive and my hope and faith in God and The Universe were there by my side.

Someone at some point did something to him that pushed him over the brink, and he totally lost his mind. He snapped and was determined to hurt a woman because a woman had hurt him, and that night I was the woman he wanted to murder. I was the release he needed to pacify the pain that was haunting and killing him inside. Did he get upset because I never said, "Hi" and I ignored him as I kept walking? I didn't really care! My guess is that he had this hatred towards women brewing inside of him for years, possibly since his childhood. All I wanted was to stay alive, and he gave me a reason to see the value of my own life once I saw how low he had stooped into his own despair and cry for help.

So, in that time and space while my eyes were closed in that dark, bottomless sinkhole...

I felt the cold metal barrel of his gun touching my right temple...

It was then that I thought this is it...

I heard the sound of him getting ready to pull the trigger...

It was then that I thought this is the end…

I held my breath and counted to 10…

It was then that I smelled the scent of burnt almonds…

I pleaded again with all my might for my life…

It was then that I said to myself, "If I must die, then so be it…"

If I died, the only consolation that came through my mind was that I wouldn't be alone in Heaven. I would have been with my mum. Either way there was nothing — absolutely nothing — that I could do. Whether I moved or didn't move, whether I uttered a word or didn't utter a word, whether I breathed or didn't breathe or even whether I closed my eyes or didn't, it didn't matter. He was in my face, and he had me pinned to the ground. He was pointing a gun to my head and he if he wanted to, he could have shot me either way before my next breath within a split second.

While I tried to breathe into my next breath during the longest and worst 10 minutes of my life, he suddenly saw some flashing lights coming from the street and quickly moved away from me and disappeared. As I crawled out of the bushes, my body was still shaking. I slowly managed to get myself into an upright position while I walked three steps backwards facing that dark circle in disbelief and horror. With each step, I stared at the imprint of the outline of my body in the dirt. I knew then I was leaving behind my old self buried in that dark, sinkhole of death. I knew… I would never be the same.

I turned around and walked towards the sidewalk as fast as I could, and it was then that I saw the flashing lights of two police cars parked at the end of Key Bridge. Although I managed to walk out of the bushes and the dirt physically unharmed, now I was mentally traumatized and scarred for life. I couldn't stop shaking. My face was covered in dirt and soaked in tears. The white coat was no longer white. It was stained by the dirt of death.

When the two police officers saw me, they immediately came to my rescue and released their police dog, a German Shephard, to search for my attacker. They searched and searched, but they weren't able to track him down. I will never understand how he disappeared so fast.

I was taken to the nearest police station in Arlington, and I followed through with their procedure the best way I could to file a report. I asked the officers who rescued me, "What made you stop? How did you see me?" They said, "We saw something big and white moving in the bushes?" They saw... my white coat! God and The Universe guided me to the white coat for a reason. Now, it all made sense. This was why I was so relentless and emotional about buying the white down coat. The white coat saved my life!

A wake-up call

The night I was attacked I asked myself the same question over and over, "Why? Why did I need to go through this as if I haven't been through enough?" The answer that came through for me was that it was a warning — a wake-up call.

Deep down inside of me I was angry at the world, at God and life itself — angry that my life had changed 360 degrees and that I was forced into a life away from home and into survival mode without any skills to survive with. Although several years had gone by since my mother's death, I still felt her absence. Something had been taken away from me and nobody would ever be able to fill that hole. I made a choice, and it was the wrong choice because I didn't care enough about myself. I was just going with the flow and was doing what I needed to do to just survive and that was it. I was lost like a leaf in the wind!

For one night I subconsciously let my guard down and although something inside told me not to cross the bridge from Georgetown to Arlington, I did it anyway. Maybe I did it on purpose? Maybe I was looking for a way out of this thing called life. In retrospect, I know I didn't value my life enough to protect myself. I always had someone do that for me, so I sabotaged the value of my own life because I felt there was no one around who cared enough, not even myself. I should have paid attention and I should have been more aware. I should have! I should have! I should have! But I didn't!

I didn't listen to my intuition — that quiet little voice within us that doesn't use words and that we so often doubt and ignore. God and The Universe were trying to tell me something and I was naive, stubborn, young, and stupid to pay attention. I simply didn't listen to my own intuition, and I ignored the signs. I took life for granted, and I was lost in life's rubble!

I didn't value my life until I realized that on the night that I was attacked that my next breath could be my last one. My warning was that I needed to appreciate life — my own life — that I needed to take care of myself to be able to find my life purpose and live it. If I didn't look after myself, nobody else would. It took someone to attack me with a gun for me to wake-up and breathe life back into my soul, into my being. I needed to heal and see my value.

Healing happens over time

The healing process is crucial because it allows us to recuperate the pieces of our old self. Once this happens, we can be compassionate and forgiving towards others. Above all, we need to forgive ourselves first before we forgive anyone else.

For months after the traumatic event, I couldn't cross a bridge. Whenever I would see a bridge, I would mentally and physically freeze. Anxiety would kick in as I felt I was reliving the whole thing all over again. I was suffering from some form of post-traumatic stress disorder. I became paranoid about anyone walking behind me to the point where I would constantly turn my head around and step aside to let them walk in front of me.

It took me years to get over this fear of people walking anywhere near my personal space. I used to have nightmares after the attack, and I had to go to therapy to overcome my fears of being outside in public or crossing a bridge, whether it was on foot or inside a car. Until one day I told myself that it was time I faced the fear, so I decided to cross a bridge on my own. It helped and my fears have gradually vanished. However, I am not a fan of crowds, and my sense of my surroundings is always on high alert till this day.

My attacker put me through unnecessary trauma because I allowed it to happen by letting my guard down and putting myself in the wrong place at the wrong time. However, after my grueling experience I

made an effort to make sense out of the fact that whether I lived or died that my life had been under the control of a sociopath for the longest 10 minutes of my life.

I knew that anger, resentment, and hatred are like poison. Negative emotions can eat you up inside and eventually make you sick. I didn't want to get sick and live the rest of my life under this dark, heavy cloud so I had to figure out a way to release it and let it go because otherwise it was going to kill me. I didn't need my attacker to make me feel like my life didn't have value. I had done that to myself already. So, I flipped the script and used the anger I felt towards him as a tool to push myself out of survival mode, rise above it and live my life purpose. By flipping the script, I allowed time to become one of my healing tools.

Time is the most immediate friend that we have to begin the healing process but like with any healing it doesn't happen overnight nor with the passage of time alone. Healing happens over time when it's accompanied by something specific along the way, such as making a conscientious effort to make the inner healing happen. You have to be ready to do the deep inner work within yourself to be able to identify and understand the root cause of your own wounds before the pathway to true healing and forgiveness can open up.

The power of forgiveness

Forgiveness is one of the first steps to healing so that you can allow love back into your life and be able to love yourself and others. It's a gift that you give yourself to set yourself free and a chance for a new beginning. Forgiveness is a way to leave the past behind so that you can open the pathway to allow and attract good things to flow with ease back into your life.

They say to always forgive but never forget because if we forget, we risk going through the same experience all over again. With time I have learned to accept what happened, to live with the scars, to understand that we are all here for a purpose, to forgive my attacker and myself, to heal, to learn from my mistakes and to appreciate the gift of life, but I will never forget.

However, forgiving and healing go hand-in-hand — one cannot happen without the other. When we forgive, we learn from our mistakes. Although the wounds will never heal completely, they heal enough so that we can move on and hopefully someday share our story and help someone else heal. It is only then that we are able to heal those wounds, so they don't come back to haunt us and we can move on with our lives. This is when we realize that our life hasn't been in vain and that it has more value than what we will ever truly understand.

When we realize that we're not in this rollercoaster called life just for ourselves but to help others along the way, that's when we truly learn to appreciate the invaluable gift of life itself and the accumulation of knowledge and experiences that are ours to share. It's our responsibility to share them, whether they're positive or negative, so that others can learn from them as well, and so that we can make a difference in someone's life and save a life. Otherwise, all our experiences will have been in vain.

The day we stop being there for each other will be the end of humanity as we know it because we cannot survive as a species without supporting each other — without extending the love in our heart through either a helping hand, kind words, compassion, acts of kindness, forgiveness, gratitude, love, or any combination thereof. So yes, it is about us as individuals but at the same time it's not. The human connection is vital for our survival.

We all need to have a deep bond — someone who listens, someone who sees us, someone who cares, someone who acknowledges us, someone who values us, someone who shows compassion, kindness, love and gratitude and someone who is forgiving as we all make mistakes. But of all the human emotions, the strongest of them all is love.

Love in the end is all there is and what makes the world go round. Love is the deep connection that keeps the essence of our humanity alive.

The gift of life

I am grateful for the gift of life.

I am grateful for my daughter.

I am grateful for my friends.

I am grateful for God's love and The Universe.

I am grateful to be able to breathe with ease.

I am grateful for Mother Earth and her beauty.

I am grateful for the Animal Kingdom.

I am grateful that I am able to look at the blue sky, the clouds, the moon, and the stars.

I am grateful that I am able to feel the warmth of the sun on my skin.

I am grateful that I am able to laugh and love.

I am grateful that I am able to listen to the birds sing.

I am grateful that I am able to look at the trees sway back and forth with the wind.

I am grateful that I am able to witness the change of seasons every year.

I am grateful that I am able to smell the ocean breeze.

I am grateful that I am able to smell the roses.

I am grateful that I am able to feel the wind.

I am grateful that I am able to see a sunset and a sunrise each day.

I am grateful for life itself and for you as you're reading my story.

I am grateful for all this and so much more...

Every breath I take every day is a constant reminder of the precious gift of life. Breathing life into the darkness that was around me that night was what kept me alive. I will never forget what happened, and I learned that in order for me to be able to continue living my life that it was important for me to forgive my attacker and myself for not valuing my own life the way my mother and my father did. I am grateful for each day that I am alive! I am grateful that I am able to breathe in the scent of life — not "the scent of burnt almonds."

Compassion, forgiveness, these are the real, ultimate sources of power for peace and success in life.

— Tenzin Gyatso, The 14th Dalai Lama —

Virginia is the founder of Virginia Earl Ghostwriting, Editing and Translating Services, Seven Mystic Rings and Translations Unlimited South America (TUSA). She has over 25 years of experience in the publishing industry and has worked at major international publishing houses from the East Coast to the West Coast writing, editing, and managing production.

Virginia has an extensive editorial background and an eagle's eye for detail. She has traveled as far as the Amazon to interview the CEO of Coca-Cola.

Aside from specializing in ghostwriting, editing, and proofreading, she also translates books to help authors expand their audience by reaching international markets.

Virginia is also the author of many books that have received #1 International Best Selling Author status.

One of her claims to fame is translating the subtitles of the first *Shrek* movie into Portuguese.

Under her spiritual business, Seven Mystic Rings, she helps her clients release their negative emotions by identifying the root causes of their blockages, fears and past traumas so they're able to move into a space of clarity, forgiveness and healing that will open a pathway to inner peace and allow for positive changes to impact their lives.

Being listed in *Who's Who Among Hispanic Americans and Who's Who of American Women*, shows her extraordinary contributions. Virginia is a recipient of She Inspires Me Awards (SIMA), London; Ambassador of the Year Award, Murrieta/Wildomar Chamber of Commerce; U.S. Presidential Lifetime Achievement Award; Lady in Blue Sapphire Game Changer Award; GSFE Humanitarian Award; Women Appreciating Women (WAW)

Hall of Fame Award, London; and U.S. Presidential Volunteer Service Award.

Virginia lives in Southern California and loves to travel to exotic places that have port wine and dark gourmet chocolate. She is currently working on her upcoming book and may be contacted via her two Facebook handles "Virginia Earl Editor," "Spiritual Healer Virginia Earl" or by visiting www.sevenmysticrings.com www.virginiaearl.com and www.translationsunlimitedsa.com

Nicole Fournier Farrell

Loving your Haters

by Nicole Fournier Farrell

Here I was on a beautiful Sunday afternoon. It was around 1 PM and I had just finished running my first half Marathon.

I was so elated, happy, and felt a sense euphoria. Then all hell broke loose.

My name is Nicole, I am the 10th child in a family of seventeen children, no twins. My father was extremely strict with us, wouldn't you be too? We learned to sit and listen and to do as he said, no matter what. We never questioned our father's words or comments. We never dreamed of it.

I got married at the tender age of eighteen and was accused of being pregnant by one of my siblings. She didn't believe me, but we had our first child 11 months after we were married. Of course, I had to send a copy of the newspaper clipping with the birth announcement to that sibling. She never mentioned it again after that. Six years later, we had another child, and then two more. We were a happy family of six living in a dream world. We were a one income family, which was not unusual in the 70's. and 80's. We were always buying the "yellow brand" meaning a step below the store brand, no problem at all.

I was a happy-go-lucky mother and wife when my youngest daughter started school in the early eighties. I suddenly found myself in an empty nest. Some of the moms were volunteering at the school so, I thought I would join them.

I used to play the guitar (just a few chords) and play the Beatles songs; Let It Be, A Hard Day's Night, and some Everly Brothers, such as All I have to do is Dream, the kids loved it, so did my daughter Amy.

The principal and teachers said they needed help at the office, so I did some work there as well. I made Dittos for the student's homework. Do you remember the copying machine with purple ink? I can still remember that smell! It's a nostalgic aroma. It takes me back to the early school days with my kids. I only worked a few hours during the day, 3 times a week. I had plenty of time to do my housework and laundry and make a full hot meal with dessert. I never missed. It was easy I was happy. Those are very fond memories of my very first job as a volunteer in my life, it was the beginning of what I love to do.

On a beautiful sunny day, after a few hours at the school, I went on home, it was within walking distance about 10 minutes. I was skipping along with my daughter Amy feeling fulfilled. I entered the house and Amy stayed outside to play with her friends. I knew that my husband Robert was home, he was sitting in his lazy boy he didn't greet me even after I said, "Hi baby, how was your day?", he looked at me with very COLD eyes. I was wondering what's wrong with him??? I've never seen him look like that before. He gets up then he said come with me, so I followed him to the laundry room, which is only a few feet away from the kitchen. I followed him along then he closes the door, I thought "Oh my God what is going on?" Then he proceeded to stretch his arm upward, (no he didn't hit me) he pointed his finger to the corner of the door and to the ceiling, he said, "Look at that." I said, "Look at What?" he said, "do you see the cobweb up there?" I replied, "oh yes, it's a little cobweb.... And!?" "Cobwebs should not be there." He said, "You find time to work at the school, but you are neglecting our home. If you need to work, think about working in our own home. You need to stay home and do your job; you need to be a better housekeeper." That hurt!

I said, "I can't believe what you are saying what you are saying! The house is clean, beds are made, the meals are always cooked on time. I love my few hours at the school. Our little girl loves seeing me in a different environment, and she is proud to have her mother there. It makes me feel good to do things outside our home. Its fulfilling."

A few days went on, I don't know why, but I started to feel guilty because I'm used to doing as he says just like I did with my father. We didn't ask questions about what our husband or dad said, it was "Yes sir, yes dad," all my life!

From then on, every time I left the house to go to school, I made sure the house was in spic and span shape, to have a really clean home, so that my husband would have no reasons to complain because I wasn't home for a few hours. After that fiasco, as I was walking home 10 minutes away feeling stressed. I thought Is he going to find a dime-sized dirty spot on the carpet or a dirty fork somewhere outside of the kitchen? Instead of being myself, "Happy go lucky Nicole," I was stressed thinking about how when I was at the school I was appreciated. I was hoping he would not be mad when I returned home.

As I am writing this, I am so sad. What was I thinking letting him treat me like that? He made me feel insecure. I wish I could erase the sad memories. As a homemaker, mother, and wife, I've had a lot of fulfilling times in my life. I made most of my daughter's clothes. I would make dresses, pantsuits with matching dresses for all 3 of my girls. I even made clothes for my firstborn son.

One year, there was a fashion show, at the girl's school. I asked if I could use some of the homemade clothes that I had made for my daughters. They were reluctant to allow me to do that. They had to have a special meeting to approve my homemade fashion, sight unseen, they almost turn me down! Well, it was approved. My three daughters' outfits were a hit! I had lots of requests for me to make clothes for the mothers, I don't remember if their father (Robert) attended. He hardly got involved in school activities, Parents night, or PTA activities.

Another flashback is having a nice dinner in a party of 10 including my ex-husbands family members. I cooked a chuck roast on a charcoal grill just outside on the back porch. That roast came out so tender and juicy they could not believe that it was cooked on a charcoal grill by me. During that party, I served all the drinks, on top of preparing the whole meal by myself. The kicker is it was expected of me. I didn't think anything of it. It was my job, that's how I was raised. My opinion is that my ex-husbands mom felt that way too. She did everything for her husband. He was the man of the house, He just sat there "not helping." Well, they did work all week and bring home a paycheck. I put up with this for years! He never changed a diaper. He "didn't know better."

All of my daughters remember that very well, but it was the "norm" then in our family circle. They saw me as their mom, and after 24 years with their father, I decided that the way he was treating me, was not acceptable. Keep in mind, he never hit me, never, it was not acceptable. They chose model husbands. They realized it's not the norm for one parent to do most of the domestic jobs. Their husbands all help around the house. They cook and change diapers. I am so proud of them.

I had three brothers in California. My Brother Joe had his Real Estate license. He had bought a home and he married his real estate agent, Maria. We got together often as they only lived a few miles away. We would talk Real Estate. One day about a year after Joe got his license, he approached me and planted a seed. They said "with your personality we think you would love real estate. You're outgoing and we know that you would be successful." I replied, "Oh no, not me." Never, are you kidding me? They assured me that I could and that I would love it. Married at 18 years old and now having 4 kids, I have no experience with the outside world, no thank you I could never do that. Well, somehow my brother Joe and Maria convinced me to go for it.

A few weeks later I was studying very hard for my real estate exam. Joe would check up on me occasionally to make sure I was studying. Later on, after so many hours of grueling study, I did finish my exam. My brother Joe assured me, not to worry if I don't pass right away. Not too many people do. He convinced me to study harder. I was determined to pass on the first try. It was very difficult for me as I wasn't used to studying. I was accustomed to being a good wife and mother paying little attention to my personal needs for years. I knew my brother believed in me so, I had to do this for me.

My husband at the time was doing his own thing. he had a full-time job and was an accomplished musician. His style reminded me of Chet Atkin. Robert was often working on weekend nights or could be found tinkering in the garage. He was and still is an accomplished guitarist. I never took that away from him. He played for hours I praised him for it, but when I had a goal of being a Real Estate Agent, he didn't pay any attention. I studied very hard.

The day arrived, I went to the mailbox and nervously pressed the big brown envelope against my chest. I walked into the driveway and went into the house. I was too nervous to open it yet as I was thinking the negative, there was no way I would pass on the first try. My heart was pounding so hard. I sat at the kitchen table all alone, the kids were in school and Robert was at work. I slowly pulled out the letter from the real estate exam office. What do I see in big red letters their CONGRATULATIONS, WELCOME TO THE REAL ESTATE WORLD. It took my breath away plus there was a big X to confirm that I had passed with flying colors. I was jumping up and down. I was thrilled!

I called up my brother Joe and his wife Maria to say that I had something to tell them in person. They rushed to our house, and we celebrated. They could not believe it! What puzzles me is that I remember my sister-in-law and my brother Joe's reaction, but I don't remember my Ex's reaction at all, even though we lived, ate, and slept in the same house. I'll never know how he felt then about successfully passing my real estate license exam. His future action will tell it all.

My brother Joe and Maria assisted me in getting my own desk at a Century 21 office where they both worked. Their broker Larry was so proud to have me join their office. I wish my Ex would have been as proud of my accomplishments as everyone else around me.

(A little resentment started to set in)

I loved my real estate work; I became the top-selling agent of our office within 6 months. In this case, though, I really want to give credit to Robert because his boss was looking for a home and he recommended me to find him a home. He better have! His boss,

Mr. Simpson, had a nice job, a good income, and good credit. He was the perfect buyer.

I did work hard for him, and he was a very difficult person to work with. He had an angry personality. He was very demanding. I was thinking, not too fast Mister, not you too! I was reminded how Robert liked to boss me around as well. Please be nice to me, I won't take it! I was strong and professional. I used kindness. I was firm and positive, and he eventually calmed down. I refused to let him get to me. No, thank you. He had a lot of demands for his dream house. It was not easy; well, nothing is easy right? Being strong, cool, and collected helped me consummate the sale. Yes, I found him his dream home within 2 weeks. It was all worth it, I learned from my past experience with life from living with my Ex. Thank you, dear!

Of course, working in a real estate office, we can expect to have a weekly meeting which was at 7 pm. My Ex-husband didn't want me to attend those meetings. He said, "Just sell houses and come home. Work a few hours a day then, when I'm home you have to be home with me. We always ate at 5 pm sharp, so by 7 PM I was free. You see he was mama's boy with old traditions. The woman stays home to serve her man. It was all about him. He was so needy, just like his father, that's the only way he knew how to react as a husband. He would not let me grow. Even though I was over 40 years old. I felt like he didn't want me to blossom. He kept me in a cocoon, treating me like an 18-year-old.

I told my broker that Robert did not want to let me go to my meetings. He said "Well, let's invite him so he won't feel so insecure." So, my Ex did come to my meeting so that he could see that it wasn't a social event. Other agents were asking me, "Why does he want to attend your meeting?" It was so embarrassing.

I acted like I was his property. I still respected him, I never talked back, and I did everything for him. Like I mentioned before, even at our own barbeques or parties I served everybody. He never lifted a finger, he'd basically shake the ice in his empty drink, and I'd run to him to refill it.

I was ok with that until we visited some friends several times and that was not the way it was at their houses. The men helped out I thought "Wow. he's so nice." I learned as the years went by, that it wasn't right. and I started to feel resentment towards him.

Our real estate office was really active with the community events and there was a 5 k (a little over 6 miles) coming up in 6 weeks in our little town. My sister-in-law Maria brought it to my attention, and I thought no way I could never do that. I am not used to being in public like that. I had never taken part in a race before. My Ex didn't like the idea at all. He wanted me all to himself at all hours when he was home.

Maria was not pushy, but she was encouraging me to join the running team. She told me, "It doesn't matter if you finish or not, it's a community affair. Our real estate company is joining as a group with our Century 21 logo." that made me make up my mind. Our kids could join in as well. I said, "yes!"

Well, the next day despite my husband's approval. I decided to take part in the community 5k run, with our children who loved it. It was a personal thing for me too. I went out and bought my first pair of tennis shoes, in 10 years. I started running in the morning before going to work making sure I did my housework,

"My duties." He really didn't like for me to do that. I was his property and he wanted me home!

I trained for 6 weeks, and I thought, "Yes, I can do this." The fact that we can either run or walk, no problem. My 3 daughters joined the 1 K walk. It made it all about feeling good, family time, and mingling with our community.

On the day of the race, our kids were all ready to walk the 2 k. It was a little over one mile. To my surprise Robert joined in to do the 2 k with the kids. This made us all surprised, we exchanged high fives, it was a good moment. The race began. I was with Maria for the 5 k along with our office team. When we finished, I found out that Robert could not finish the one-mile run. His knees were giving him problems. We gave him a big hug for trying, we truly felt bad for him.

Days went by and life went on as usual. I kept on doing my daily chores. I continued working feeling successful in raising our children and being a Real Estate Agent. I tried my best to be home at night when he was home. I did a lot of 5ks (over 6 miles) feeling so good. I also kept the house in tip-top shape!

One glorious morning changed my life. It was the day that I finished my first half marathon, which was a little over 13 miles. Good grief! It was one of my biggest achievements, giving birth to our four children. I was on cloud nine, feeling so good, and euphoria is the best word to describe it. I almost quit so many times during the course of the race, but you know what? Runners support each other and give each other encouragement even if we have never seen them before. They keep us going saying things like, "You got this, you're almost there! Don't quit now! You know, maybe that's why I became so addicted to running. It was like a magnet that pulled me to more races. I had "support" from complete strangers. Now 40 years later, I am reliving those moments and yes it makes sense. I needed to run to fill a void in my life.

After finishing the Marathon, my daughter Amy helped me a fill up a large pan of warm water with Epson salt. Oh my! When I took off my running shoes, "ouch!" I noticed that I was losing my toenails, all of them. I didn't have the proper running shoes. As I was running, the top of my shoes would constantly "hit" the top of my toes, but I was happy. That took the real physical pain away somehow.

I was sitting outside in my "rock maple rocking chair," just like the one my mom used to sit in after a long day's work. That chair has sentimental value to me, it's close to my heart.

The weather outside was so perfect it was about 80 degrees, I just sat there feeling the breeze at high noon. It felt, so good even though I was in pain. As I was soaking my feet and rocking gently, I was focusing on the cool breeze on my face, the wind in my hair, and then reality set in!

Robert came home from work. I was excited I couldn't wait to tell him about my half Marathon. I did it! I finished the race! He walked a few feet past me, I was still in my running clothes and seeing that I am soaking my feet in a bucket of water, I said, "Hi honey with excitement in my voice," he didn't reply. He kept on walking. He went into the house and after two minutes, he returned with a stern look on his face. He pointed toward the back door where he came out from, I said, "what's the matter?" He had an angry look on his face, then pointing for me to get in the house he said. "You didn't make the bed this morning."

I could not believe my ears so, I got brave and spoke. "Well, you were asleep when I left, why didn't you make the bed?" Oh man, he got really angry, not because the bed wasn't made but because I talked back to him…, he got really mad and he shouted, "If I was meant to make my own bed, I would not have gotten married." Oh wow, it all came together, he thought that I was his servant. Things were never the same after that. I lost respect for him.

We went to a marriage counselor. First, we tried a female therapist. After the first session, Robert said, "I'm not going back." but he tried. Then, we tried a male therapist, but that still did not work. He could not admit that he was wrong.

He was raised that way. It's what he knew. He didn't know better. I don't hate him. I feel bad for him.

I filed for divorce about a year later. I'm not 18 anymore, I grew up.

Belinda Foster

Overcoming the Trauma of Bullying

by Belinda Foster

Facing Challenges in Life

Each day is a new day full of hope and promise. I approach each day with vigor to connect with people and share special moments in dialogue and conversation with friends, family, and new people who I meet along the way. I look at the world we live in through the eyeglasses of creative empowerment and self-expression. Where there is a will, there is a way.

My closest friends and colleagues know me as an effervescent people- person. I was not always this way. The road to self-discovery, self-confidence, and empowerment was a rocky road from the start, a difficult journey that began because of traumas that occurred in my childhood years. There was a series of devastating experiences that I went through from being bullied as a child. The after-effects of these experiences derailed my self-confidence for a period that seemed like an eternity.

I want to share with you about the bullying that I faced as a child. The effects of bullying go beyond the moment of being pushed, punched, slapped, and even ridiculed in front of classmates. It is the after-effects that are the worst I believe. It was only when I could face the turmoil that occurred through tools that I learned along the way that I was able to break the bondage of the hurt, the emotional trauma, and arrive at a safe space for healing. Here is my story.

Bullying in a Digital Society

I want to start with my observation of bullying in today's society. We live in a world full of technological developments that continue to advance in speed and efficiency with respect to connecting people worldwide at any given time. We have new apps, virtual games, and software to research, learn and communicate in light speed online.

We are indeed connected with one another by our phones and devices. Sometimes bullying can occur on social media through interactions that are just as devastating as being bullied in person. Cyber bullying can lead to victims feeling humiliated on the internet, leading to feelings of despair, panic attacks and so many other forms of anxiety. I experienced these same emotions as a victim of campus bullying. I am going to address face-to-face bullying in this chapter and what it was like for me.

In writing this chapter, it is my hope to reach you with the human connection with my story that hopefully will impact you in a positive way.

Being Bullied in School

Growing up as a child, I enjoyed the art of observation. When it came to being around other kids, I was a kid who loved to observe kids who were good at speaking and communicating. I liked to learn through watching others do what I did not know how to do. I found inspiration in doing so. In fact, I liked to watch my parents and their friends have conversations with one another as well. I learned immensely in that way.

The first day of first grade was so exciting for me. In my mind, it was just as exciting as going to Disneyland. My parents had just moved to a new home near the school where they wanted me to attend. I was excited about meeting new kids in the neighborhood and especially kids at my new school.

The excitement of a new beginning is an amazing experience for a child and my parents had bought me a nice outfit for the first day of school. I felt so happy putting on new shoes and a new pantsuit to start my first day of school. During the first week, I remember meeting some nice kids in my class and a few kids in upper grades. During recess, we were talking to get to know each other and playing jump rope. Then came the day that I was eating my home-made lunch which I recall vividly. My mom had made me a peanut butter and jelly sandwich. While I sat on the bench preparing to eat my lunch with friends, I recall a girl walking up to me, a girl who I did not know. She told me to give her my sandwich. I was really surprised that she was demanding my peanut butter and jelly sandwich. I distinctly and vividly remember this girl looking at me with a mean look and laughing at me. I remember a feeling of fear in that moment. I was thinking to myself that this could not be happening over a peanut butter and jelly sandwich.

There were other kids around me, and they did not say anything or tell her to leave. They looked afraid too just like me. In that moment, I suddenly felt like I had to think of something to say. I was not sure what was happening and the next thing I know is that she snatched the sandwich from me and pushed me down off the bench I was sitting on. She took my food and ran to another bench to sit with some other older kids that were in an upper grade. I remember looking to my right at the girls on the bench where I was sitting. They helped me up and I sat shaking on the bench. I was suddenly not hungry anymore at that point. My knee was scraped, and I felt totally humiliated. I experienced a sense of embarrassment, shock, and hurt all at once for the first time in my life at the age of six. I felt helpless like I could not stand up to the girl who took my food. I also felt like a victim for the very first time in my life.

As a child, I recognized that I was afraid, and it crushed the confidence in me. I froze from being physically and psychologically abused by another kid who was much bigger than me. The next day when I came to school, I felt anxiety walking on the campus. I began to think about something positive like hoping that everything would be different the next day and that the girl who bullied me would not hurt me again. That day was smooth and calm until the next day when she did it again and slapped me in the face. The cycle of abuse continued to happen repeatedly on numerous dates and times at lunch and even when she saw me walking down the hallways in the school building. It was hard to pinpoint or sense when it would happen. Because of these encounters with her, I found myself experiencing anxiety at lunchtime not really wanting to go out on the yard to have my Lunch or to go to the cafeteria. I was so upset with myself because I was younger, shorter, and smaller than her. I could not win by trying to defend myself. School became a place of learning and also a danger zone for me.

Coping with Trauma of Bullying

The thing is I wanted to tell my parents, but I was afraid to do so. My mom would always ask why I was so hungry when I would get home from school. She would ask why I wanted a sandwich right away when I walked in the house after getting home from school. I did not want to tell her what was happening to me at school...that there was a bully who was taking my lunch and physically hitting me. I was afraid that she would hurt my mom or hurt my younger brother.

As I continued to be bullied by this same student, I began to lose my sense of self-worth and my desire to communicate with kids at school. I would carry a carton of raisins and an apple and eat that in the library where I began to go instead of on the yard with other kids. I would sneak and eat my apple in the library and nibble on raisins as I sat and read books, like Snow White and other picture driven books.

Over time, I began to dread going to the campus out of fear of what would happen next to me. I loved learning in the classroom setting so much and being around my teachers and friends but being targeted by a bully reduced me to an anxiety ridden, fearful child who was afraid of being attacked repeatedly. Over time, I found myself very fatigued during the second half of the day of school trying to work in class without eating lunch. I became so afraid of the bully coming out of nowhere and pushing me down or hitting me. It was hard to concentrate in class sometimes to take notes and even quizzes.

The thing is each time she attacked me, I felt paralyzed, and I could not do anything. Other students would not say anything to her or defend me because they were afraid of her too. I began to shut down and my confidence was shattered.

One afternoon the girl who bullied me came into the classroom, walked over to my desk, and knocked my books off my desk. I felt a sense of overwhelming fear that it was now escalating to cross over into the classroom environment. The teacher was out of the room at the time. In that moment, there was a boy by the Dominic who was sitting in front of me, and he told her to stop hitting me and knocking my books over. I felt honored because he was the first kid who stood up for me, but I was afraid of what she would do to him.

After Affects of Bullying-Fear and Anxiety

I recall one traumatic day when she walked up to me in the hall on the way to class and said that she was going to beat me up when the bell rang at the end of classes for the day. She said she was going to attack me on my way to head out of the gate leaving campus to get in my mom's car to go home. I envisioned in my mind the long route from the exit door of the school all the way across the basketball court to the gate where we exit. I felt an overwhelming anxiety about walking off campus. As the time drew closer to the end of classes for the day, my hands began to shake, and an overwhelming tension come over me. I was not trained or skilled in martial arts or any kind of self-defense. I feared for my safety and what she would do next.

My teacher came up to me in class and asked why I was shaking. I told my teacher I was not well. She walked me to the principal's office. There I sat safely until my mom came in to pick me up from there. After that day, my whole demeanor changed. I became further withdrawn, afraid to walk on the campus each morning to start the day. Some nights I had restless nights from what I went through. I kept a journal to note my experiences. I did not want to tell my mom again because I wanted to make sure they were safe from the bully.

The thing is this. It got so bad that when I would catch a cold and would have to stay home to get well, I saw that as a happy moment because I would be safe at home. Even in those moments, I continued to yearn to be educated and seek knowledge and study each day. At the same time, I was afraid of being beaten up in the school setting. I did not feel safe at school anymore because I was not safe there. This is part of what I went through that tore down my confidence, my identity and self-esteem to the point where I associated in my mind school with danger as opposed to education.

I began associating school with peril and physical abuse instead of success and self-development. The only places I knew were safe were the principal's office and the library. The librarian watched every kid like a hawk. The girl that bullied me never came to the library.

Returning to school, I had a new coping mechanism for safety. I found myself nestled at a desk in the library during lunch and recess periods where I would enjoy eating a granola bar or an apple while reading a good children's book. I did this to avoid the bully and protect myself from more physical and mental trauma.

My Search for Healing and A Safe Haven

I saw the library as my creative safe haven. I sat in a cool desk near a corner with stuffed animals where I found contentment and a place to hide away from violence on the yard. I regained a sense of feeling safe at school. Over time, I did not see the bully in the hallways of the school.

Later, I learned that the girl who bullied me transferred to another school. The damage was done even after the bully transferred. I was not the same kid anymore. I decided to stay in the library and continue my healing journey there. I was able to rise above the trauma that I went through over time, and I began to go back outside on lunch breaks to try and make new friends. I felt hesitant and anxiety walking out on the yard the first time I did this. I thought that it was my responsibility to pull myself up and regain some sort of confidence. The thing is that I did not know how to heal the pain inside of me and the emotional trauma. I soon found myself opening up again and talking with kids more in my classes. Little did I know that there were other bullies later that I would have to face.

There were moments as a kid that I found myself feeling very confused as to why I had to go through being physically abused at school by another kid. Why was this my life experience as a kid? I was little. I was not bothering anyone. I was simply trying to be nice to other kids and learn in the classroom. Why would anyone want to harm someone who they do not know and someone who has not done anything to them? It did not make sense to me. I realized that at some point I had to learn to protect myself through standing up for myself. I began voicing my feelings in a way that I felt safe to share through writing. I began to keep a journal and write down the incidents of being bullied in detail and the feelings that I had toward those attacks. I also began writing poems that I kept in my journal. Poetry about the power of fear, breaking down the sound of silence, and the pain of hurt. Poetry about abuse.

It took a while to heal. A long while. I can tell you that. The experience of going through all of this was like walking through fire. I fought my way back through writing poetry and journaling. I fought my way back in my solitude of learning as a quiet child that was quieted by trauma. My education now became a tool not only for self-development and learning but more importantly for self-healing. I grasped every aspect of my English class, diving into paragraph and poetry structure. Reading the works of great authors at an early age. I escaped into the world of literature like poetry by Emily Dickinson, Jessica Greenbaum, Emma Lazarus,

Robert Frost, and Edgar Allen Poe. I soon developed an armor of strength through embracing their literature and seeing myself as a survivor and not a victim anymore. I was numb from fear at this point. I had enough numbness to fight to rise above the trauma. I realized that a person can only take so much even as a child like me.

I soon grew to become taller in stature, more importantly stronger in my mind set that there was always a way to figure out a problem and to find a solution.

Being bullied was a horrible experience. It did change me in so many ways as a kid and growing up through my elementary, middle, and high school years.

Yet, I realized that I could find my way to healing and overcome it all to become new.

Trauma changes people. The thing is we either fall by it or we rise above it. I wanted to be like Batgirl or one of the Fantastic 4 and rise above it overnight like watching a good superhero movie. That is the thing I want to share with you here. I found myself fascinated with these movies in my youth development. It was because I could relate to Clark Kent being off to himself as a reporter and turning into a superhero to save others. I saw it as a lesson that we can learn to save others with our gifts and even save ourselves when we have a problem or challenge. It is about figuring out how.

When I got to second grade, I did share with my mom what happened to me in first grade. She told me that she wanted me to promise to tell her if anything else happened. I told her I did not want the bully to hurt her. Then, suddenly my mom shared that she too was bullied. We found synergy in that moment, and I recognized something. Yes, I was a little kid, and my mom was a kid once too. She is my hero in so many ways and I was relieved that I could finally open up and share my trauma with her.

Another thing that happened was that I met a friend in school who stood up for me to another bully who had threatened to beat me up in fourth grade. At that point, I was emotionally numb because I was finding my path in coping with the original trauma. Feelings like fear were dealt with through the power of the pen. I began to not fear the feeling of fear and it showed to the next bully. I found the courage to stay calm in my facial expression and not show fear in my eyes even though my knees were shaking. This time was different. A friend jumped in front of me and stood up for me. That moment I will never forget. The new bully left me alone from that day forward. The friend that stood up for me became my best friend throughout elementary, middle, and high school years and even today. I realized that to find joy in life and to find the happiness in life that I so wanted especially as a child, I had to first face that there are nice kids and there are bullies. I did not know bullies and the physical abuse they unleash on a victim existed until I started school. I learned over time to face the fear and tackle it with my new ability to stay calm in the moment and look in their eyes with no fear. I was taller and stronger. I learned to write from taking English classes which became a tool for my healing. Each time I went through trauma, I would write another poem or prose.

Through writing and reflecting on my life experiences as a child, I soon learned how to accept what happened and then overcome fear head on. It took time because being afraid on a level like that represents traumatic fear. There were so many emotions that came up when I was victimized by my attacker, I had to process them over time to reduce them in intensity which was a result of putting in the work. I continued to share with my mom my experiences as well. This helped me rise up and together she and I worked on putting back together the broken pieces of me.

Experiencing Healing and Renewal of Self-Confidence

One day I arrived at healing. I woke up one day and felt free of fear. I began to see the bullies that hurt me not as antagonists but as human beings who just used their energies in the wrong way to hurt people, they felt they could overpower. I decided to take the power back and that was when something changed in me, like Maya Angelo penned, "And Still I Rise." Each day I rise through the struggle. I feel like a soldier who fought and won a war that I did not sign up for.

I want you to know this. You have the power to always make a choice. I changed my perception of my inaction. I no longer saw myself as a coward for not fighting back physically when I was attacked at school as a child. I began to celebrate my choice of nonviolence. I was able to do that when I read about the Diary of Anne Frank and other great works that showed how heroes like Anne fought to maintain her integrity through writing in the midst of trauma and chaos in her environment. I also found strength from Martin Luther King's letter from a Birmingham jail and other great works that depict challenges people have faced in the human condition.

You can set a goal in your mind and heart to work to overcome the fear of bullying realizing that you have the power within you. You have the permission to change your perspective in how you see yourself, a bully, and the trauma you have gone through in being a victim of bullying. Bullies come in all shapes, sizes, and can appear in both work and school environments. In the process of healing, you transform from being the victim to becoming the victor over the trauma through acceptance of what happened, communication with a mentor, and knowing that you have the tools within you to survive it. Will power, faith, hope, and tenacity are the tools for survival of trauma like this. Then over time things change... over time... for the better... and you awaken to a new you. A stronger, wiser, and a new beginning in life. As for me, I grew up to become a mentor for kids, youth, and adults who have gone through bullying and other traumas in their life, and I continue to do so even today. The healing process you must know is not automatic. It takes time. Give yourself time. Love yourself. Share your trauma with someone who cares. You will find strength and healing over time. All it takes is one person to care. I hope I have helped you with my experience and sharing with you today.

"Where there's hope, there's life. It fills us with fresh courage and makes us strong again...." ~ Anne Frank

Stephanie The Shopologist

The Secret to Loving yourself

by Stephanie The Shopologist

You can Win Big in the Game of Life by learning how to Master the Art of Loving Yourself and Your Haters at the same time. It is through the same experiences that you can approach challenges brought to you much like you would a variation of the game of Sudoku.

Sudoku Rule No 1: Use Numbers 1-9,
Sudoku Rule No 2: Don't Repeat Any numbers
Sudoku Rule No 3: Don't Guess
Sudoku Rule No 4: Use Process of Elimination
Sudoku Rule No 5: Don't Ever Give up

Learning to Love Yourself and Your Haters is complicated and can be compared to playing a game of logic and reasoning, just like Sudoku. If you don't know what number to put in a certain space, keep scanning the other areas of the grid until you see an opportunity to place a number. But don't try to force anything - Sudoku rewards patience, insight, and recognition of patterns not blind luck or guessing. The game is infinitely varied, with millions of possible number combinations and a wide range of levels of difficulty. It is all based on the simple principles of using numbers 1-9, filling in the blank spaces based on deductive reasoning, and never repeating any numbers within each square, row or column.

We are raising the future world leaders in the Digital Online Transacting Revolution. Life requires multidimensional flexibility and extensions of grace towards others. In Life and business, it is more important than ever to Be YOU, Brand Yourself, Stand up, Stand out, and Lead by example. In sharing your Gifts and Talents with others, becoming a positive difference maker in the world, you will definitely bring out the haters. They will focus directly on YOU through social media and every other platform they can find to attempt to blow your light out.

Rhinoceros Success by Scott Alexander is a great book to help keep your light shining while loving yourself and your haters through the storms. It encourages you to go for the NO, and to find daily success in failure is Rhinoceros Success by Scott Alexander. It reminds you that you are born customized to complete your unique life's journey. Haters will show up to give you practice in the areas you need improvement and to teach you how to find the good in every bad situation. They help you recognize that you are an endangered species, just like the Rhino. The darts of haters cannot penetrate thick Rhino skin and they will just roll off as if nothing happened. Rhino's get up in the morning, polish their horn and charge the day wearing the armor of LOVE, the helmet of salvation, shield of faith, belt of truth, boots of readiness, peace, and the sword of the word. Speak life. Speak hope and victory into yourself and your haters. Complete every challenge that presents itself during the day with Gratitude.

The most successful people in the world, have failed the most and have the highest EQs in the world. They could not have accomplished their life's purpose without having the interference of their haters and most learned to be grateful for their participation. I believe that by sharing our gifts and talents with each other and leading by example we can help the haters replace their hate with love and gratitude. One act of kindness at a time.

Change the Way You Think about Yourself

You are probably familiar with self-help books and talk show hosts who tell you to love yourself, but you may be wondering how to go about that. While your relationship with yourself is the most important connection in your life, it's easy to forget about nurturing it and it is even more difficult to love and appreciate your haters.

However, self-love and compassion are too important to neglect because they shape your experiences and relationships with others.

Protect your health and wellbeing by making positive changes in your Mindset and treat yourself the way you want people to treat those you love.

Maybe you're hard on yourself or you're so busy with external obligations that you rarely consider your personal priorities. Looking inward could help you to value yourself more.

These strategies will help you to think more highly of yourself:

- Accept yourself. Know that you are worthy of love and respect just the way you are in this moment. Embrace yourself with all your strengths and weaknesses.

- Clarify your purpose. Invent your own definition of success. Ask yourself what a meaningful life means to you, even if that answer changes over time.

- Talk yourself up. How do you speak to yourself? Choose words that are encouraging and uplifting. Use your internal dialogue to build your confidence and manage your emotions.

- Offer forgiveness. Let go of the past so that you can move on. Take any decisions that you regret and turn them into opportunities to learn from. Make amends where possible and resolve to handle things more constructively in the future.

- Avoid comparisons. Facebook didn't invent social comparisons, but social media has increased the potential for envy and inferiority complexes. Try competing with your last performance instead of living up to someone else's standards. You'll accomplish more if you dare to be yourself.

- Think positive. Looking on the bright side and being able to laugh at yourself makes you even more loveable. It also helps you to manage stress and deal with difficult circumstances.

Change the Way, You Treat Yourself

Do your actions match your beliefs? You might say you love yourself, but your actions could be sending a different message.

Try these techniques to treat yourself with kindness:

- Practice self-care. Develop habits that keep your mind and body fit and strong. Go to bed early and exercise each day. Eat a balanced diet and watch your weight.

- Pick friends wisely. Surround yourself with family and friends who encourage and support you. Cultivate close relationships with others who share your goals. Engage in deep conversations where you can share your feelings and receive validation.

- Pursue your passions. Identify the activities that bring you joy and fulfillment. Block out time each day for something you love, whether it's a task related to your job or something you do in your leisure time.

- Set goals. Give yourself something to strive for. Working towards realistic and challenging goals builds your confidence as you add to your achievements.

- Maintain boundaries. Know your limits so you can define what behavior you consider acceptable. That may include physical boundaries such as needing your own space and psychological boundaries such as being entitled to your own feelings and opinions.

- Advocate for yourself. Once you understand your needs, you can communicate them to others. You'll grow more skillful as you practice being direct and tactful in letting someone know if they cross your boundaries.

- Seek support. Ask for what you need. Let others know specifically what they can do, whether you're looking for practical assistance like pitching in with housework or just a friendly ear to listen while you sort out your feelings.

Loving yourself can help you to enjoy more happiness, overcome challenges, and build healthier relationships with others. Make it a habit to treat yourself and your haters with kindness and respect.

Loving yourself and your haters is a journey, not an event. Be coachable and teachable. By forgiving yourself and others it will help you win the power keys of life that open special doors, full of supernatural gifts just for you. When you think about the family you were born into, the people who you influence & that influence you, the situations that become repetitive and those that don't, it becomes clear that we keep getting opportunities to learn the lessons we need to learn and master. This amazing Game of Life, by Design, presents you with a lot of choices, challenges, and unexpected changes that require you to spin on a dime. Be coachable, teachable, quick to forgive and willing to keep a Mindset of gratitude. Stay in gratitude through the good, bad and the ugly times. When you are able to Master the Art of Loving Yourself and Your Haters. That is when the Magic Happens and Supernatural gifts are delivered!

It is not always easy to identify haters. Sometimes they are right under your nose and are the most important haters you get to have in your life. They are also known as your "Sandpaper People," picked out especially for you. They help sand off rough edges of your developing personality, smooth out any jagged perspectives and/or change your life's direction completely by providing the constant sanding required to completely change the shape of a specific area of your life to help you. Help enough others get what they want so that you will have what you want. Hindsight is 20/20 and when you learn that "Sandpaper People" are part of your Life by Design, they are often times in your life required for you to go from Good to Great.

Every person in the world is born with a special gift that only they can activate and share with others. The family you are born to and the people who come into your life forever or for only a season are sent to help you identify it, activate it, love it, and share it. People who have not discovered their gift, are often told they do not have a gift and are probably in environments that consistently tell them what they can't do. Some people instead of what they can do may choose to do the same thing to the people in their family and to the people who come into their life. It is very important to remember "IT IS NOT WHAT HAPPENS TO YOU THAT MATTERS......IT IS WHAT YOU DO WITH IT".

If you were taught to be a hater, you do not have to continue to be a hater. You can break the chains and become a positive difference maker by changing your mindset. All you have to do is Say Yes To yourself and figure it out with all the other positive difference makers. Your choice of breaking the hater chains will start bringing healing to you. Start Now, Choose to Change your mindset, forgive those who hurt you and identify the gifts that your haters have. Watch how the universe releases supernatural love, prosperity and unmatchable grace for you and your future generations.

My gift is connecting & promoting entrepreneurs who want to share their gifts and talents to roll out smart cities to access over 16 million customers and get attention from meta influencers in 52 countries who specialize in building shop local communities that turn haters into people who love themselves and their haters. Learning from the 7-figure earning Go To Guys and Girls who have done it. They are winning in the Game of Life by sharing Love and Gratitude. They have learned the secret to keeping great blood flow and cashflow, so you can enjoy life in an extraordinary way.

I am excited and honored to be able to share some of these golden nuggets that I have personally used to learn how to love myself and my haters. I'm grateful for the lessons their actions helped me learn and the 10x income they helped me generate by sharing my experiences with them to help others.

Stephanie the Shopologist

Founder of Ask the Shopologist & The Go To Guys & Girls Get Paid Academy

Do you have a business looking for customers and/or do you want to learn how to Monetize your product or service creating additional streams of revenue to your bottom line? :)

I have a wealth of new possibilities we can explore together Creating Your Custom Plan!

Reach out Now and Let's Get Started - WOOHOO - Here We Go!!!

Asktheshopologist.com

Raven Hilden

Your Haters Can Make You Greater!

by Raven Hilden

Have you ever been told that you cannot do something? How did it make you feel? Did you feel defeated? Perhaps not good enough? Or did you let it drive you to do great things?

I have found that those who tell you that you cannot do something are reflecting on their past experiences or perceived lack of ability to do it. Or perhaps they are fearful of their loss when you achieve those goals. We all have varied backgrounds, gifts, tenacity and determination. What might work for one person might be a disaster for another. And even if things don't work out in the beginning, you can try again as now you know what doesn't work!

There is a story about a baby elephant. This elephant was sold to a circus to be used in circus acts. He was treated very poorly and beaten. The elephant wished desperately to be free. Every day this elephant was tied by a rope to a small post so it couldn't leave. Shortly after, the elephant tried to escape to a better life by tugging on the rope. For days he tugged and tugged. Eventually, he gave up and decided that he would forever be tethered to the post.

Many years later, this elephant was still tied by a rope to the same small post. However, the elephant was now much older and much, much bigger! The same sad, depressed elephant didn't know that it now had the strength and power to simply pull at the rope and walk away. It had tried to leave many years ago and felt defeated. Instead of trying again, it submitted to a life of despair. Life is too short to stay in one spot!

We all have the power and ability to free ourselves of the things that hold us back. Some goals seem like an impossible and daunting task but in hindsight, we had all the tools available to us. And the strength. After all, strength is not the absence of fear – it is facing that fear and not giving up.

Facing obstacles or difficult times is always much more difficult alone. It is so important to find those who cheer for you and talk about you behind your

back – in a good way! Negative people will often try to make you feel guilty for being happy. Haters come in all ages, genders, and can even be family or a 'friend'. Most of the time, haters are reacting to an unresolved conflict within themselves. Very little actually has to do with you. I found it very important to remove haters from my life or create as large of a distance as possible. There is no benefit to keeping haters in your life and haters should be a part of your past, not your future.

I was exposed to very toxic environments when I was younger. Oftentimes I felt as if I was responsible for the way others felt. It took years for me to look inward and deal with the pain and guilt that I felt. I also felt like a victim and blamed my faults on those who hurt me. It wasn't until I realized that if I can blame my negative faults on someone from my past, that I can also blame the positive influence haters had on me too. Although I did not deserve the things that had happened to me, it did make me stronger, more empathetic and resilient. It gave me a drive to help others without expectation and a passion to support others. I am thankful for that! I can't say I love my haters, but I can say that my haters have made me greater!

I decided to channel my pain and passion to create a nonprofit to serve others. In the beginning, I didn't really know how it would turn out, but I was determined to learn. I had people tell me that it wouldn't be possible. That I didn't have enough money. That I would burn out and quit within a few years. I must say that I have overcome all of those obstacles and continue to grow!

At first, I kind of felt like maybe I wasn't good enough. I was told that most of my life and like the elephant, I began to believe that my dreams weren't possible. But something kept driving me like a fire in my soul. I had to do it. I wasn't completely sure how I would make it happen, but I would give everything I had to try. After all, it wasn't about helping a million people, even helping one would make a difference. I knew I could do that!

The nonprofit that I started - MilVet.org is now very successful. We have won many awards and I have a great team that is the backbone of the organization. Awards and recognition do not drive me. The accolades do not inspire me. What keeps me going is seeing the difference that I am able to make in the life of a homeless veteran, a child, a single mother, a struggling senior. It is seeing one of my volunteers succeed and do things

that they did not think was possible. I thrive on encouraging others to see the best in themselves and challenge the worst. I am successful when I have helped another person avoid some of the pain I have felt.

One of the best things I did to start overcoming some of my self-defeating habits was seek new opportunities and try them. I learned that I had to do things differently in order to achieve something new. Otherwise, we end up with the same results, right? A pivotal time in my life was realizing that in order to gain some things, I also needed to leave some things. I quit watching movies and stopped surrounding myself with people who did not support my goals and dreams. I declined a few barbecues to study and had to re-evaluate how I was spending my time. Looking back, I spend too much time with those who hindered my growth and drained my happiness. That could have been time learning something new, meeting new people who share my passions and making memories with loved ones.

Growth and happiness really happen when we find the people that make you greater, who believe in you and inspire you to grow. There will be people who are afraid of your growth – it might change their life. Then again, it just might change yours!

Learning from our mistakes is a normal part of life. Everyone makes them. Sometimes they are big and sometimes they are small. The important thing is to learn from them and move on. Mistakes do not define who we are. No matter what your past was, you can move forward and be a better you. We aren't in competition with anyone else, just on a quest to always be a better version of ourselves. After all, we have experienced different things, different places, etc. I believe that every person has a special gift and experiences that can change the life for someone else. Sometimes, that gift can change the lives of many or even create a shift in how society perceives things. Remember, we don't inspire others by being perfect, we inspire them by the way we deal with our imperfections. We all make mistakes, but our strength is shown in the way we overcome them and get back up.

When we make a change in someone, whether it be a spark, a difference in the way they view the world or themselves, or inspire them to act on their passion, it creates a ripple effect. That person just might inspire another person to make a change, and so forth. The results can be amazing!

Another way to make an even large change is through mentorship. Having a mentor is huge. My first mentor was a woman who believed in me and gave me a chance. She saw something in me that I did not see yet. She encouraged me to learn more, to reach outside of my comfort zone, and to keep going when things got rough. I am forever grateful for her. Since then, I make sure to learn from those who have achieved something I aspire to do, or that I look up to. No matter how much we think we know, there is always more to learn.

Just as it is very important to find a mentor, it is equally as important to become a mentor. You have learned something that another person might really love to know. Or maybe you have overcome something and can help someone else through their journey. We all have something to give. When we give to others, it always comes back around, and we are blessed in return. Sometimes isn't immediate, but it will happen. Oftentimes, the best gift is just believing in someone else and encouraging them to grow and succeed.

Over the years I have seen many miracles of change happen. One of my volunteers was struggling with the loss of a loved one. He was very depressed and was having a hard time finding happiness or purpose in even the smallest things. I asked him if he would like to assist with the nonprofit's holiday program and he reluctantly agreed. Our holiday program provides gifts to children of veterans who are in great need. Some of them are ill, some lost a parent and others are homeless. This was in the year 2020 when covid shut everything down. MilVet was delivering gifts and food to families as locations were closed. I asked our volunteer to help me deliver to a family that was homeless. They lost their house after the grandfather, a Vietnam veteran, became ill with stage 4 cancer due to agent orange. The grandmother was still working to help pay for a motel for the family and their 14-year-old grandson lived with them.

When we donated the gifts, the grandmother began sobbing and tearfully explained that the family was not going to have anything for the boy for the holidays or a hot meal. As we walked away, my volunteer looked at me and said, "What the hell have I been complaining about?" It definitely gave him a different appreciation for the plight of others and a purpose. He was a veteran as well, so giving back to others was healing for him. This does not mean that he didn't have struggles or miss his wife but helping others has a way of helping ourselves in the process. We are meant to give back to make the world a better place, even in the darkest of our days.

I am grateful for the opportunities that I have had and the people that helped me grow along the way. I would not be where I am without those who give their time and talents to me, the organization and those we serve. I believe that angels walk among us, as I have seen them in action.

A final thought since this book is about haters. Don't be one! Sometimes people don't realize that they are being a bit judgmental or less encouraging than they can be, or silent in a time of need. One of the worst things we can do is be silent in a time where our voice is so important. We can all take a look inside of us and see if there is something that we can improve upon or someone we can reach out to when others are not. Be a beacon of hope for someone who is in need of guidance in a journey that you have already navigated. Share what you have learned and make someone else's journey a bit easier. Step up when someone is being wronged. Encourage someone who needs extra light and love. The goal is to leave the world a bit better than when we arrived.

"We might not change the world for everyone, but we just might change the world for one."

Raven Hilden

Founder/CEO MilVet

ceo@milvet.org

Melissa Kahn

Love your Haters

by Melissa Kahn

Nothing average or normal has made a difference in the world! It is human nature to follow trends and desire what others have. We all want more, we also all want to be appreciated and liked. But rising up and achieving more and becoming unique and amazing all comes with a strong amount of jealousy and hate. Being unique and different isn't always fun, and being a leader comes with so many obstacles. Being strong and innovative doesn't mean the others around you are the same, nor does it mean others will support, follow or appreciate your work. In life it takes tremendous achievements and wealth for people to listen and follow your guidance. No one climbs to the top without a glitch, not to mention that very few that have risen to the top were ever labeled as normal before their achievements. In fact, most of the most influential people who have made a difference were considered weird, nerdy, odd, too much, or straight up insane. Achievement and success don't come without a lot of hate, setbacks, failures and judgement. It is human nature to judge and to feel jealous of others doing well. All these comments and judgement each of us feel along our journey hurts. Sometimes it hurts to the point that it sets us back and dulls our electrifying energy and desire to move forward. But what if you took all that hate and turned it into growth building?

The most important thing I have learned on my journey towards success, is not everyone will like you no matter how hard you try. The road least traveled is often the most criticized. It is human nature to dislike and argue, hence it is very common in life to come across many bumps. It is natural to distant yourself from people that are not in agreement with you. Other misfortunes come as barriers like anger, jealousy, meanness, along with love support and comradery. We can continue to work for acceptance and support, or we can work towards being on the top and make a difference. Being the best and working hard to get there can often be lonely and achieving the highest award doesn't always earn you supporters or friends. In life you have to decide where you want to be and what you can handle. On the journey to the top, so many emotions and haters can derail you, if you accept this or take it personally it will only pull you down. It is our responsibility as an individual to learn to channel these haters into life lessons of growth. It is our responsibility to learn and become even stronger and better by the feedback and the hurt that others do to us.

Okay I know that sounds crazy and nearly impossible, but we have never really mastered any skill in life without failing. You didn't start walking without first falling. We learned every way it didn't work before we finally figured out what actually worked. Learning this lifelong skill as a baby took many steps to achieve the goal, it took us holding our head on our own, to rolling over, followed by pushing ourselves up with our arms, then finally starting to crawl, followed by pulling up to stand, all before we ever took that first step. That first step was not the end of all the failures rather more falls and disappointments to follow. We don't personally remember that journey, but we have been part of other loved one's journey and witnessed the frustration and hurt from falling. What if as an infant we acted like we do sometimes as an adult and just give up? What if we never got frustrated enough or independent enough to want to walk? Can you imagine if we could keep that child-like determination as an adult? Remember when we would do something just because our parents told us it wasn't possible, or we couldn't? Remember when working to achieve something didn't involve someone else's judgement? Most importantly remember when our parents and teachers would tell us that someone was just jealous when they were mean to us.

If you want to take your power back and you want to become the person you dream of becoming, you have to reestablish that child-like determination and tenacity to rise above your haters. You have to turn that hate into fuel to be the best and make the difference you were born to do! From a young child I was teased or hated on because of my undeniable determination. I was told things came easy to me because I was pretty, because I came from a wonder family with all the right contacts, and because my family was well known. I was constantly trying to friend people and give or do anything for anyone to make them like me and appreciate me for my heart and love for others. It took years for me to realize anyone that I had to really try to get to like me was just not my tribe, and they were only setting me back. Once I started into my adult life and building my career, I quickly realized I would never get to the top by being friends with everyone. Now this doesn't mean I wasn't friendly and helpful to all my colleagues, but I realized sharing my personal feelings and emotions would only make me weak and give others power over me. This was a very hard and lonely time for me because I had always talked to everyone about everything, and now I had to relearn how to communicate professionally and ethically while still building a healthy business relationship.

Learning how to communicate through a healthy business mindset changed everything for me. It prevented me from constantly giving people information that they could use against me out of shear meanness. It made others respect me more, which in return taught me to value and respect myself. It taught me how to have friends and colleagues, so I didn't expose myself to humiliation. But most importantly, it taught me how to make my career and my work place an enjoyable and prosperous place. Whenever I walked into my office it was my heaven away from any personal issues, it was my place to shine, it was my place to be the person I wanted others to know me as. My workplace is my happy place where drama and emotions cannot enter, because I am there to work and build my empire and anyone that isn't there to be a part of it isn't allowed in my circle to dim my light. Keeping my emotional stress and drama at the door, created healthy relationships and tremendous productivity, it also set an example for others, so it quickly became a happy productive place for everyone if they chose to. Learning not to talk about any of my employees or colleagues' personal life or misfortune was the best thing I have ever learned! Majority of us have guilty conscience so when we speak bad words about others it effects our peace as much as theirs and the overall environment.

If being mean or speaking hateful things effects our peace and hurts others, why do we continue to do it? It's a cycle and it often makes us think we feel better about ourselves when we speak out loud something bad about someone else. It makes one feel powerful and above others. When we feel down or failure is in sight, we make excuses and blame others. No one likes to be wrong! But at one point or another we all have been wrong simply because we haven't learned the "right" just yet. What I can tell you is even if you do everything perfect and you put all these tools into practice, you still will have someone from time to time hating on you...why?? Because they are failing and need someone to blame, because they are unhappy and can only find comments related to jealousy. It isn't our job to hold on to these hateful comments and actions, it's our job to acknowledge the situation and shine light on the ones hating and move forward in a positive way to keep on track with what we are put on this earth to accomplish. We have to keep moving to make a difference in the world!

One has to learn lessons from hate! I always take hateful comments in a productive way, meaning in a context I can help grow and make myself or my business better. If you lose yourself in anger or depression from hate, you let the haters win and you strip yourself of peace, growth and prosperity. Every hateful comment has some sort of anger or hurtful feelings related to it which can

keep transferring and destroying or it can be used to learn and better yourself. Often when you clash with opposition and jealousy, it impacts everyone, but the approach of kindness, forgiveness and understanding will channel the criticism and negativity to a positive healthier outcome. Hate will consume your time and energy. Your opponent may continue their self-destructive path while your wise decision making is nothing but less stress, more fruitful decisions. Mindset is everything when dealing with haters and sustaining self-love. Sometimes the message is hard to understand, sometimes it simply means you are being a leader and people less motivated are jealous and want what you have. Sometimes it means they are battling hurt and anger and just repeating what has been said to them. So we can either learn or grow from hateful conduct, or we can acknowledge that we are doing things right because we are climbing to the top while others are choosing the downward road of anger and hate.

Yes, I will say proudly I have chosen a different path than majority, I chose the high road of loving the haters to overcome their failures and prosperity of my struggles. Learning to be compassionate and open minded will not only benefit the people around you but will help you with your inner peace and happiness. Most importantly though, learning how to understand haters and their motives will only give you the most honest explanation of what you are doing right or what you need to adjust. Always offering positive energy and forgiveness will be the only thing to truly heal the situation and yourself, and don't ever shrink to someone else's level because they don't feel confident.

Dr. Cherilyn Lee

My Journey...
Forgiving the Unforgivable!!!!

by Dr. Cherilyn Lee

Forgiving is one of the most elusive, misunderstood, and life-altering concepts. Many people believe it means forgetting what happened or condoning bad behavior, but forgiveness is giving up hope for a better past. Forgiveness doesn't change the truth, imply the pain didn't hurt, allow unfair justice or reward the betrayer with another opportunity to leap back into the relationship, but it does develop a path for your journey. It is common for feelings of retaliation to occur. It doesn't make you an awful person. If those feelings arise, you need to be honest with another person to release the scorn or desire for vengeance associated with the malicious behavior. If you don't express how something made you feel, it will make you sick. It's normal to feel hurt or angry, but how you deal with those feelings will determine your quality of life, health, and future. Forgiveness, or lack of forgiveness, will either trigger additional problems or propel you forward with even more conviction to have a happy, healthy, prosperous life.

Forgiving is a journey, not a destination. It takes time and encompasses letting go of things you have no control over, which can result in becoming immobilized by painful feelings and memories. Science has proven that grief and trauma travel through our DNA, affecting our health and well-being. When you hold negative energy inside, it converts to toxins running through your veins. Not being able to forgive produces damaging chemicals that flood the body with stress hormones and harmful neurotransmitters that flow throughout all of your organs and systems in the body. Suppressing resentments and not forgiving produces symptoms and issues like blurred vision, diabetes, stomach aches, headaches, heartache, chest pain, joint pain, high blood pressure, cancer, etc. Lack of forgiveness suffocates rational thoughts and emotions, causing devastating righteous behavior. It reminds me of an analogy I once heard: Holding onto resentments and not being willing to forgive is like drinking poison and hoping the person I hate will die. You may never understand why someone did something to you, but you still have to forgive all who've wronged you, even the violent, depraved predators who did something horrific to you, such as rape or causing a loved one's death.

You can't allow the circumstances surrounding an incident to block you from moving past the inexcusable deplorable actions or wanting to seek revenge. Don't feel guilty if you think about getting even; just don't act on it because it will only come back to hurt you. If you can't forgive, your life will be governed by an endless cycle of resentment and retaliation, so do not let wounds linger. Denying these feelings or holding onto a grudge will keep you stuck in the past and prevent you from progressing with your life. Moving past this pain can feel like a hopeless battle; however, please keep in mind that you will be able to recover with time and transcend the pain. Holding on to the past and letting go is a conscious decision. Can you imagine how much free time and energy you would have throughout the day to focus on your mission and dreams if your negative emotions did not hijack your life?

Forgiveness does not mean you have to see your abuser or predator face-to-face. You can let go of grievances by writing a letter to release whoever injured you, even if you don't mail it. It gives you the opportunity to share what you experienced without being interrupted or contradicted. It's vital that you have the chance to express exactly what is bothering you, so memories of the despicable betrayal don't trap you in an endless cycle of distress. The other person's explanations and apologies may have meaning and benefit, but their excuses are not part of the process for you to personally, unequivocally forgive. It's pretty common to dwell on the disgraceful conduct instead of letting it fade into memory. Even after your existing contempt passes, sometimes it takes a lot of soul searching to let go absolutely. Forgiveness does not always happen immediately just because you want to let go. You can't control the past, but you can choose to love yourself and heal your inner trauma, so you don't keep repeating and reliving it. People struggle with self-love because they cannot forgive themselves or others and continue to blame themselves long after the trauma has passed. Developing acceptance, self-love, self-forgiveness, and self-compassion is a step-by-step process and is essential before truly forgiving or loving anyone else. I know this to be true because I was a victim, held myself hostage, and did not want to let go.

Forgiveness is about choosing to live a life without letting others have power over you and not letting unresolved anger and bitterness dominate your life. Remember, someone else's decision to hurt you is never your fault. It helps to describe your unwanted feelings on paper. Writing kinetically releases it from the fabric of your DNA. It's impossible to change the past, no matter what, so you must accept what has happened. Then you need humility to learn, grow and change your inner thought life to manifest a life you love while being a blessing to others. It helps to create a positive mantra to counter painful thoughts. I always wear a badge that says, "I am so grateful that I am a Magnet for Miracles."

How you talk to yourself can either assist you in moving forward or keep you glued to the past. Having a mantra, you tell yourself in times of emotional pain, can often help you reframe your thoughts. Although this process is not always easy, the results can be spectacular, like a caterpillar morphing into a butterfly; you transform from living in misery to evolving as your true authentic self, finding peace, and knowing boundless new freedom. Remember, forgiving is for you, not the person who violated you. While forgiving may help others, above all, it has unlimited benefits for you, most notably allowing you to heal and revolutionize your life.

I had to come to terms with the painful experiences I endured, from the childhood bullying and the threat of my legs being amputated to the failed marriage, the battle with pulmonary embolisms, the comas, being homeless—and many other trials and tribulations. Despite all these traumatic experiences, I learned to forgive others, especially myself. Forgiveness does not happen overnight, but it is a road that we all must navigate. It's a necessary way of life if you sincerely want to heal. Otherwise, every aspect of your life will continue to be adversely affected.

EMOTIONAL ABANDONMENT FROM MY FATHER AND STEPFATHER

I don't ever recall feeling loved by my stepfather or my birth father, who was totally absent from my life. My biological father and my mom divorced soon after I was born. When I was two years old, my mother remarried, and now I had a stepfather. Four years later, my half-sister came along, and she was perfect in every way, unlike me. She was beautiful with flawless skin, and her body was completely healthy, unlike mine. My stepfather never treated me the same as my sister, his biological daughter.

His narcissistic behavior hurt me in countless ways over the years, including damaging my lungs permanently for life.

On one occasion in elementary school, I remember walking up to my stepfather and asking him for 10 cents. It was a sunny afternoon, and I wanted to go to the little neighborhood store around the corner. My stepfather stood up and looked down at me and told me, "I don't have any money for you," he said it so matter of factly. The way his voice sounded, I believed him as if he did not have any money. There was not a harsh tone in his voice. I didn't feel sad at the time and accepted that I could not go to the store.

As I began walking away, my little sister walked up to her dad and asked him to give her 10 cents. Before I could leave the room, expecting him to tell her the same thing he told me, without any hesitation and knowing I was still in the room, he reached into his pocket. At that precise moment, I turned around, looked at him, and watched him pull a dime out of his pocket and hand it to her. She was so excited and thanked him profusely. I felt as if I was sucker-punched in the gut. It was a huge shock that jolted me to the core of my body. How could he give her a dime and tell me he had nothing for me? I was categorically and utterly devastated. After that, I knew from the depth of my life that I would never ask a man for money or anything else again.

My stepfather would continuously smoke cigarettes inside the car and in the house, knowing I had asthma. He would even lie to my mother about smoking in the house, and she believed him. He would literally leave me gasping for air, wondering if I would die on many occasions, as I was often rushed to the hospital. Many times, I thought to myself, "This is it; this is really it. I can't breathe. I am going to die," because I was not allowed to complain or speak up. Like a typical child, I suppressed the trauma and emotional pain, which created many illnesses.

What hurt me the most out of the countless unconscionable transgressions he did to me over the years was that my stepfather refused to allow me to carry his last name. As a teenager, my mother let it slip that she had asked him to adopt me so I could have the same last name as everyone else in the family, and he was firmly against it. He did not want me to have his last name or for anyone to think I was his daughter. The rejection and abandonment made me feel like I was cursed and not part of the family. It made me wish I was never born.

FORGIVING MY STEPFATHER
STARTING MY HEALING

The perpetual neglect, injustice, and unfairness throughout my life unquestionably affected me emotionally, influencing all aspects of my life. The beliefs and perceptions you develop as a child seep into your subconscious and influence every thought, decision, choice, and action which shapes your health, relationships, career, and destiny. Shame destroys your self-esteem, causing you to think you are worthless, inadequate, or unwanted. It diminishes your true sense of dignity and erodes your belief that you are a deserving, valuable, lovable child. These faulty beliefs can lead to an overwhelming flood of negative self-talk as well as self-defeating. People should be counselled toward forgiveness and emotional healing. I follow this approach because of my own childhood. If people learned to make peace with their inner turmoil, which produces physical ailments, far fewer people would be living on prescription drugs trying to manage their painful physical conditions.

I tried forgiving my stepfather multiple times throughout the years. I can't begin to express how difficult it was trying to forgive him, but I knew holding onto the hatred was just making me feel worse and keeping me sick. So, I kept writing about forgiving him. I would also recite over and over; I forgive you for all the pain, suffering, and irrefutable damage you did to my health and body. It was not until he passed away that I could forgive him entirely. When I forgave him, I felt new freedom as the bondage shackling me was released, and an overwhelming surge of energy flowed throughout my mind and body.

CHILDHOOD EMOTIONAL SCARS

Repairing the damage to my skin started with finding ways to forgive the children who bullied me. Not only was I suffering at home, but I was also ridiculed at school for my appearance. I felt all alone from the bullying and did not want to live anymore. I never felt safe at home, school, or had anywhere I could go to find a little relief from the constant abuse in every direction. At school, the kids singled me out because my skin looked different. Although bullying doesn't always take the form of physical violence, the kids threw rocks and dirt at me. They pushed me down and taunted me with names like raccoon or lizard girl because the skin around my eyes and mouth was rough, dry, peeling, dark, and scaly. My mother searched everywhere to try to locate various prescriptions and ointments, but nothing helped because my skin was beyond inflamed. My eczema became so bad that the infected sores would ooze, while the dried, cracked top layer of my skin would bend and rub inside the creases of my legs, ankles, feet, arms, neck, and face.

I couldn't stop myself from scratching because the itching was fervently intense. So, when I scratched it, I would get weepy sores and hyperpigmentation on the skin, appearing darker in spots. My skin complexion was always blotchy, never even. It looked like I was at least three distinctive color tones at all times. My legs were such a bloody mess down to the bone that the doctors at the hospital actually scheduled an amputation to remove both of my legs. Initially, they thought the eczema was a kind of MRSA, a flesh-eating disease, since I had very little skin left protecting my nerves and muscles, and I was running a high fever.

The internal infection rapidly spread, and my white blood cell count was dangerously elevated. I nearly lost my legs because the doctors didn't know what to do about my endless intense itching and scratching. They felt I would wind up with deadly infections that would take my life, so they believed it was safer for my legs to be amputated. I am eternally grateful that they ultimately did not remove my legs at the very last moment. One merciful doctor of the seven doctors refused and created a solution to heal the infection. He kept submerging my body into a whirlpool and then took me out after so many minutes. He'd pat me dry and take me back to the room, and a few hours later, he would submerge me in again. The treatment went on for several weeks, along with new dietary restrictions. He is the reason I wanted to become a doctor. He was the first man to treat me with kindness, decency, and dignity. As I was leaving the hospital, I knew in my spirit that I wanted to be like that empathetic doctor who saved my legs from being amputated.

In my case, eczema had its roots in emotional pain, like most patients who suffer from eczema and other chronic conditions. I couldn't forgive the kids while they were tormenting me in elementary school because I felt isolated, lonely, and depressed without any hope. When I was older, I understood that children often try to impress their peers. Most children are selfish and do not understand what they are doing and how their unconscious behavior impacts others. Many adults still behave that way until they heal their childhood wounds. They only care about their own end game and what benefits them without regard to whom they must step on to get there. Decades later, one of the girls I went to elementary school with passed away. We were in contact when she transitioned, so I attended her funeral.

HOW I FORGAVE THE BULLYING

As I was driving to her service, all the agonizing memories of the kids who humiliated me in elementary school poured back to me. I started visualizing each of their faces while driving down the highway. I would see Sally's face and say aloud, "I forgive you, Sally. Then I would picture Billy's face, and then I would repeat out loud, I forgive you, Billy." I named just a few since so many of the kids in my school dreadfully tormented me. I went through each of their names because I knew they would show up at her funeral and I would run into them. When I walked through the door, they were so happy to see me. It was as if they had no clue what they had put me through. I carried their mistreatment toward me around like a ball and chain for years. Yet, they appeared to have no memories of it or had forgotten all about it! My pathway toward forgiveness was put into motion on the day of her memorial as I began to forgive one person after another.

While forgiving others, I had to go through every layer, like peeling an onion. Authenticity is mandatory for forgiveness because forcing yourself to forgive doesn't benefit anyone, specifically yourself, if you're still holding on to pain and indignation. I had to go within myself and internalize forgiveness. Then I would visualize each face. Then I could start forgiving every person out loud. "I forgive you, Lucy." Then I would imagine Johnny's face and say, "I forgive you, Johnny." I was slowly chiseling away at my hatred because I realized my health would continue to deteriorate if I held onto these grievances.

Releasing resentments is a lifelong process. Every day, just like brushing your teeth, I continue to chip away at it because annoyances are always ongoing. If it builds up over time, the consequences can be irreversible. Irritations happen daily, so we have to keep forgiving. It's necessary to let go of circumstances like people hurting your feelings, forgetting to pay you, not keeping their word, cutting you off in traffic, or children not appreciating the sacrifices you have made for them. Each time you let go of a resentment is like dropping another heavy rock you dragged around everywhere you went. Eventually, you will start to notice that you are feeling lighter. Situations keep occurring all the time, so you have to continually be in a mode of forgiveness.

EMOTIONAL SCARS FROM TEENAGE DISAPPOINTMENTS

Although my biological father was absent most of my life, he would emerge once in a great while and then leave me again with even more wreckage than before. My father promised to make up for all the times he let me down. He said he would buy me a car for my high school graduation present so I could go off to the university. After filling out paperwork for a scholarship, my father didn't come through with the car. Naturally, I was disappointed that I didn't have transportation, which meant my dream of attending the university was shattered. The car symbolized my freedom as I juggled school and 48 hours of work.

After graduation, I was still living at home with my mother, stepfather, two sisters, and two brothers, so I enrolled at the local Junior College (JC) and started summer school. Soon after, my stepfather had a job-related accident, and four of his toes were severed. He was in the hospital for several months and then back and forth to rehab for nearly a year. He had to learn to walk again. I was saving all my money from work to purchase a car since I took the bus everywhere. My mother told me that my stepfather would be getting a large settlement. She asked me to hold off from buying a car at this time and wanted to borrow my savings in the bank and hand over my entire paycheck each week to her. She said she needed me to cover all the household bills and expenses, including the food for seven people. She promised me that they would repay me and purchase a car for me once he received the settlement.

About two years later, they finally received the settlement. That day, I left the house as usual at 6 AM for the JC and returned home at 11:30 PM after my typical 8-hour shift at work from 3 to 11 PM. When I got home, I saw their brand-new family car in the driveway. As I walked in the door, I noticed the entire house was full of brand-new furniture. Bags of new clothes for everyone in the family were lying around all over the place since they had been trying on all their new outfits. They shopped till they dropped. Most of my clothes growing up always came from second-hand stores. I asked my mother if we could get my car the next day. She told me they had already spent every last penny and could not get me a car, and there was also no money left over to repay me for the money I loaned them.

HOW I FORGAVE MY PARENTS

Unfortunately, many people are fueled by their own self-interest, even when it comes to their very own flesh and blood. Acceptance was the key to forgiving my parents, but it did not occur overnight. I forgave my parents because that is who they are, and their selfish, self-seeking behavior had nothing to do with me. I know the sooner you can let go of the things you can't change, the sooner you will free your energy allowing a new solution to come forth. Man's rejection is God's new re-direction. I realized I had to use this as my opportunity to take responsibility for my life and start the process of learning to love myself, which took years to ultimately grasp.

MY FORMER SPOUSE

I continued attending the JC, carrying a full load of classes, and still worked the same long 48 hours a week. I was determined to succeed without the help of a man, as I painfully had learned from my stepfather as a little girl. If my parents had kept their word and bought me a car as promised, I would never have met my ex or had my beloved children. While waiting at the bus stop one afternoon, the gentleman who owned the local furniture store asked me where I was going every day as I always used this same route. Then he asked me to lunch and drove me home. I shared my aspirations to attend medical school and my profound desire to become a physician. He was the first person that wanted to hear my thoughts about what I wanted to do with my career. He was very kind and caring. In just a few short months, we married when I was only 19, and he was 26 years old.

We were married for eleven years and had three beautiful daughters together, each being 11 months apart in age. He was wonderful in many ways, always supportive of my education, and was very good to our girls. However, he was a major cheater. I constantly noticed things like lipstick on his shorts, and I did not own or wear any make-up. I also observed obvious hickeys on his fair-skinned neck. When I confronted him, he claimed it was an allergic reaction to strawberries that he had eaten earlier that day. I let it go because I knew he would lie about it, and I didn't have any energy left over for a fight because I was so busy from the time the sun came up until way after midnight between school and homework while raising our three little girls.

After eleven years of marriage, I wanted a divorce, so I asked him to go to the courthouse and file the necessary papers. I thought he was my husband, but we discovered we were never officially married when he filed for divorce because we forgot to send in the marriage certificate. That is actually more common than you think. So, I will just refer to him as my ex. Years later, when I forgave my ex, I started feeling the heavy fog clouding my brain dissipate. Then I woke up early

one morning marveling at the pink and orange hues gleaming from the sunrise and realized I was beginning to feel good again. I wake up so happy, filled with joy because I learned the recipe for happiness: acceptance, letting go, forgiveness, and self-love. I realized this is my journey, not my destination, as this is an ongoing process.

One day, my daughter told me that I had never forgiven her father, my ex. I argued with her because I really believed that I had forgiven him. Then God revealed to me that I had not forgiven him. I know God gave me a test when my ex asked me to borrow money to pay his second ex-wife's rent. When he specified it was for her, I felt my blood pressure rise. That's when I realized that if I had forgiven him, my body's physiology would not have responded like that.

God forced me to undergo the lessons I needed to learn. I suddenly recognized that I was holding onto a grudge without ever noticing that it was inside of me escalating this entire time. The long-standing indignation left my blood pressure unstable during that time. After a moment of clarity, I let go of the animosity and understood the hostility was only causing me harm, not him, and I was able to set him free.

FORGIVING MY FORMER SPOUSE

If I had held on to the bitterness, I would have gone down the other road, a horrible self-destructive path, and I would not be here today. I learned how to heal myself with forgiveness. If I didn't forgive my ex, I would've ended up with colon cancer because my CEA blood tests were rising, and my loathing was so ingrained that it would have festered throughout my colon. Knowing he was having various affairs was always haunting me. Forgiving him was easier said than done because my extreme hostility knew no bounds.

Experts believe that forgiving an ex can allow you to break the cycle of pain, move ahead with your life, and embrace healthier, loving relationships after a break-up or divorce. Rebuilding a partnership takes time and effort to re-establish the broken trust. If your partner suffers from sexual addiction, it needs to be treated as an illness so both parties can fully recover effectively whether or not they choose to remain a couple. Discovering that a partner has cheated on you can be a crushing revelation. I understand forgiveness can be difficult if they had an affair with someone you know who's close to you, had a child with another person, or promised you they wouldn't do it again and continued to cheat. You still need to forgive, or you will never be happy and at peace with yourself.

Our thoughts, cells, and even subatomic particles carry tiny electrical energy. Stress and thoughts of retaliation produce erratic vibrations that lead to disharmony, injury, and disease. Forgiveness does not mean reconciliation, letting someone off the hook, or giving up claims to a fair settlement. Six years later, after my divorce, I took my ex to lunch and shared with him that I had forgiven him for the past pain and hurt. Then he told me that he had never done anything to anyone that would ever cause him to need any forgiveness.

Forgiving your ex doesn't mean you have to be friends, but it does mean that it is finally time to meet your best friend, who is yourself and look in the mirror. I recommend that my clients look into their own eyes in the mirror. No matter how uncomfortable it is, you need to do this exercise in the mirror, looking into your own eyes. This exercise has helped me extraordinarily throughout my journey. Give yourself permission to try it for 30 days consecutively. If you do this as prescribed, you will be happier about life and receive mental clarity, self-confidence, serenity, and peace of mind. The benefits of doing this 30-day exercise are priceless.

You need to say, "I love you. I love myself just as I am. I am peace. I am love. I am joy. I am loved by God. I am grateful and blessed for another day. Every cell in my body is healing and vibrating for optimum wellness. I am living prosperity consciousness. I am living infinite possibilities. I am living empowerment. I am wildly wealthy. I am prosperity in action now. I am manifesting divine support for my financial abundance. I am manifesting multiple streams of passive income. I am magnetizing abundance so it may flow into me and flow through me for the benefit of all. I am safe. I am open and willing to experience mental, physical, and spiritual healing. Amen!"

Every morning and evening, wrap your hands around both sides of your upper arms like you are giving yourself a big hug, and say to yourself, I love myself unconditionally, then say I love you... (fill in your own name.) Repeating these words to yourself in the mirror twice a day will begin the process of loving yourself and help you create a world that you never imagined possible.

FEELING ABANDONED AND REJECTED BY MY SISTER

While I was in the hospital for 30 days, my sister did not come to visit me. I felt like she was ignoring me, and she hurt me immensely. After being released from the hospital, my pain and resentments bubbled up to the surface each time I was around her for the next seven and a half years.

HOW I FORGAVE MY SISTER

I meditated and prayed about inviting my sister to lunch to clear the air because I needed to approach her with unconditional love in my heart to heal the distance between us. Eventually, I took my sister to lunch, determined to listen with empathy, and speak with compassion. We held hands and prayed before we ate. Then I shared how I felt about her not coming to see me in the hospital and asked her why she didn't visit me. She explained that she had watched her father, my stepfather, die. She said she never wanted to see a family member that sick again and was told that I might not make it. She expressed that she couldn't stand to see me that way and wanted to remember me being whole and healthy. When she conveyed her feelings to me, it was immensely freeing. I always felt that she had neglected me when I was in the hospital, but that wasn't the case at all.

Sometimes the bad blood we're holding against people is distorted, and we've perceived it completely wrong. Often many complex factors could have played a part in their disturbing behavior. Once we had that conversation, I was able to fully release all my unnecessary pain, and it brought us closer than ever because I was willing to be open about my feelings, and she was ready to listen and be honest about hers. Realizing that hurt people often hurt people can help you cultivate compassion toward them without minimizing their actions.

If you have not healed your wounds, you can be triggered and misinterpret people's actions or misunderstand current situations only to react inappropriately to the present circumstance. Sometimes people have trouble letting go of others' mistakes. They hold onto grudges whether they are based on factual events or only imagined wrongdoings. Either way, they both come with a price. Stinking thinking continues to produce unpleasant consequences. Forgiving others and ourselves is infinitely terrifying yet necessary for achieving optimum health and authentic relationships, particularly with ourselves.

HELPING MY PATIENTS FORGIVE

At times people equate forgiveness with weakness, although the reality is exactly the opposite. It strengthens every aspect of your life. Forgiving is the key to letting go of your baggage and giving yourself and all of your loved ones the kind of future everyone deserves, but it begins with loving yourself in the present moment. When you let go of being the victim, you take charge of your life. It's okay to take baby steps to let go of the feelings. Resentments can build when people sweep things under the rug, so be vulnerable and don't bury negative emotions. I encourage you to write down three ways your hurt feelings have influenced your life. Become aware of the feelings you still experience long after the unconscionable betrayal has passed. It would be best if you found someone like a very close confidant that you can absolutely trust or a therapist to share your private thoughts and secrets to help facilitate the process of letting go and learning to forgive. Each time you release another resentment, it's like dropping a boulder weighing you down. Another resource I recommend is finding support on the various 12-step programs, especially if you do not have the money to seek professional help.

If you took an honest inventory of your shortcomings and discovered you played a part, even if it was the fact that you didn't set any boundaries in the relationship, you still need to acknowledge it. Then take responsibility for your part in the conflict or dispute. Only offer a heartfelt apology to the other person when appropriate. This will validate their feelings, promote forgiveness, and allow you both to move on. One person's ability to do this can change the dynamic of the relationship. We all affect each other's brain waves, so challenge your beliefs and self-defeating thoughts so you can choose healthier balanced relationships. If it is not plausible to have contact with them, I want you to write on a piece of paper. I release you from the pain you caused me when such and such occurred.... then describe the incident. After releasing them from the pain they caused you, now it's crucial for you to forgive yourself for holding onto the pain and hurt.

You need to know in your soul that the only love that counts and impacts your life is that of self-love and God's love. Love from everyone else is okay, but it can be temporary, and self-love and the love from God is everlasting. You can't find true love or a healthy life partner if your primary relationship is not with yourself and God. No one else can be as good to you as you can be to yourself. Find methods you enjoy to transform negative emotions into positive ones, like exercise, group meetings, jumping on a mini trampoline, meditation, prayer, therapy, yoga, being in nature, and creating art such as singing, dancing, painting, sculpting, writing, etc. Soothe hurt feelings by putting your feet on the ground (earthing) or taking a warm bath with Epsom salts. Play with animals and allow their unconditional love and positive vibrations to elevate your life condition. There's abundant science and research to validate the connection between the mind, body, and spirit today.

SWALLOWING YOUR VOICE

I like using Bach Flowers with my patients since they effectively identify and heal emotions. I customize the remedies for each individual during the session. I had a patient come in with high blood pressure and esophageal reflux. I knew she was holding onto a deep-seated resentment even though no matter how many times I tried to nudge it out of her gently, she kept insisting she had the perfect life with a loving husband and a fabulous career. But then she had an epiphany and remembered when her sister borrowed money from her. She told me that every time she saw her sister, she got sick to her stomach because her sister was always out spending money and never brought up repaying her, and she was too afraid to speak up for herself.

I explained to my client that I wanted her to go inside herself, pray, meditate, and visualize bonding with her sister. The next time she saw her sister, she needed to express how she felt and describe the stress and the physical side effects that were harming her body and mind. Two weeks later, she came in smiling at her follow-up appointment with me. I checked her blood pressure, and it was surprisingly normal. She was so thrilled and couldn't wait to tell me what had happened at lunch with her sister. Her sister had a surprise for her before she could express her feelings. Her sister said she was so grateful that she never nagged her for the money, so she bought her a brand-new car and even paid cash. As soon as she received the vehicle, suddenly the esophageal reflux problem disappeared, and it hasn't bothered her again!" If you are swallowing your feelings, you need to find a way to stop! You'd best believe there is an emotional link to every symptom and condition in our body. If you want to heal, you have to forgive.

BREAKING THE CYCLE OF PAIN

Once, a young girl in her early 20s had missed two appointments with me because her juvenile rheumatoid arthritis pain became more severe, causing her to pass out and forcing her mother to call 9-1-1. When I saw her three weeks after being discharged from the hospital, she came hobbling into my clinic with a walker because the pain was still unbearable. She and her mother were sitting in my office. Spirit led me to ask the girl what happened to her when she was 9 or 10. Her face turned red as she began to wail, "My father walked out of our house and threatened he wanted to divorce my mother. As soon as my father left, the pain started in my body."

I practice reflexology, a beneficial healing modality that addresses the entire body by deeply pressing the specific points in the feet to clear the blockages along the meridians. So, I took the girl into my treatment room and turned the lights out, leaving us in the dark. We meditated while listening to soothing healing music. I gently suggested to her, "This is what I want you to do. We're going to close our eyes. I want you to see your father and forgive him. I know that's going to be very hard!" We did a special prayer while I applied heavy pressure to the acupuncture points on her feet. In her mind, she was able to see her father's face and confront him. When she first stretched out on the massage table, she was filled with pain and agony that had been destroying her life. She envisioned herself forgiving him and letting go. As she was letting go, the tears slowly dribbled down her precious face as she wept while taking nice, slow, even deep breaths. Then the pain that was viciously riddling her body released.

I was able to facilitate and assist her spiritually in transmuting poison into healing medicine. In a short time, she claimed she was feeling much better. Before long, she was able to let go. We

were processing her emotions for over an hour. When she got up from the table, she had no pain residing in her body! She left her walker in my treatment room after just one session! She didn't need any pain medication, including pills, injections, or homeopathy. Two weeks later, she landed the ideal job and thanked me for turning her life around. About a month later, she came to see me. She only complained about minimal shoulder pain and said she never felt happier and was wholeheartedly at peace with herself.

She said she was able to let go of all the pain and anguish regarding her father and desperately searched and searched to find him. She tracked him down at his new address, where he was living out of state. She discovered that he had remarried and had three more daughters, which now means she has three sisters. Even though she knows her dad was raising those girls without her, she was able to forgive him. So, when she was finally able to connect with him in person, he came to the door and welcomed her with open arms. She was able to rekindle her relationship with him and meet her three new half-sisters. Forgiving and healing the relationship with her father allowed her to develop a genuine, caring relationship with her new family.

Everyone who walks into my office is altogether different. Some patients come to the clinic as if they're wearing their disease like a label plastered across their forehead. They are not their disease, but they have made it their identity. My number one prayer is, "God, send me the people who want to heal so I can work with them. Let me be a vessel; work through me so I can help them." As I pray, I pay homage to the sensational doctor who saved my legs and freed my mind when I was a child. Without his compassion and dedication, I may not be alive today. I ask God to help me pay it forward and find those ready to do their own internal work necessary for healing.

People need to understand the power that we have within ourselves. Your belief system can either get you into trouble or help you manifest your wildest dreams. You might think if you sleep with the window open, you're going to come down with the flu. You don't catch the flu that way; you get the flu because your immune system is weak, and thoughts directly affect the immune system. I leave home every day with my hair wet. I walk in the rain, and I don't catch the flu. I take appropriate actions to protect my health, particularly mentally, taking care of myself, which keeps my immune system healthy. Keeping the mind focused on the positive is critical for healing. Every day I say to myself, "I am healthy, and the DNA in every cell, tissue, and organ vibrates in wellness and keeps my body and mind strong. My spirit and soul vibrate with bliss, ease, joy, love, and peace, uplifting those around me."

It's imperative to do positive affirmations on a daily basis because never-ending negative thoughts change the neurotransmitters in the brain, weaken the organs and alter the 50 trillion cells in the body. According to the National Science Foundation, an average person has about 12,000 to 60,000 thoughts per day. Of those, 80% are negative, and 95% are repetitive thoughts. Cognitive Behavioral Therapists call these Automatic Negative Thoughts (ANTs). Please remember that all negative thoughts are not bad. Sometimes negative thoughts and awareness can help you survive a dangerous crisis, but most negative thoughts are useless. They only create imaginary drama in your mind.

There are ways to break this self-defeating pattern. It's essential to list every negative thought about yourself and others, including your fears, insecurities, losses, and regrets. In a separate column, I want you to write a positive for every negative thought. Changing your perspective takes constant practice as you make it a habit, and eventually, this new routine becomes a part of your subconscious. Creating a new inner monologue for yourself can free you from being glued to the past and allow you to advance in your life.

It would help if you watched your thoughts like an observer. There are basically two mental states. One is negative, and the other is positive. With negativity, you are suffering and filled with emotions such as anger, embarrassment, fear, frustration, greed, grief, guilt, inadequacy, irritability, jealousy, rage, resentment, or shame. With positivity, you glow and experience appreciation, awe, bliss, caring, creativity, ease, faith, gratitude, joy, love, and peace. Your thought life is the foundation for your destiny. The best gift you can give yourself is to improve the quality of your inner thoughts because they become words that influence actions and subsequent actions, which turn into habits, building your character and eventually leading you to your destiny.

The journey toward forgiving is a pilgrimage! While you are learning to love yourself, it can be helpful to surround yourself with people who love you unconditionally, even with your perceived flaws, to help facilitate your journey. Unfortunately, in my case, I didn't have anyone to love or support me, so it was an inside job. Forgiving permeates every nuance of your life, affects everyone around you, and can elevate humanity. We should have a holiday to celebrate forgiveness, even though every day should be a day of forgiveness. It would be a blessing if people could remember the importance of letting go of the past, being fully present in the moment, and having hope for the future; what a better world we could have. We also need to have a day to acknowledge the unconditional love of ourselves and others because love can transform an enemy into a friend. If people did that, the world would turn around, and people would heal. If people were honestly at peace within themselves, it would cause a ripple effect, and we would probably have more world peace. Hugs are also required for healing, so we could also use a day of hugs, heart to heart. What comes from the heart goes to the heart, so always hug everybody heart to heart.

Although I never became a medical doctor, I did become a Certified Natural Healthcare Professional and founded the Comprehensive Alternative Family NuWellness Healthcare Center in Marina Del Rey, California. I did receive my PhD, DD, RN, NP, and PA and offer genetic nutrition, epigenetic and heavy metal screenings, IV therapies, functional lab testing, etc. Throughout the last 38 years, I have pursued my studies in the advancement of medicine from workshops to symposiums, from leading experts amassing over 30,000 hours of knowledge. I am a multiple Lifetime Achievement Award recipient for my volunteer services from four Presidents of the United States and received numerous awards and recognition from government branches at every level, from the City Council to the State Department, for the humanitarian work I provide under my NuWellness Development Foundation, Inc. This 501(c)(3) nonprofit offers the Only Cost-Free Thermography, a Painless & Radiation Free Breast Cancer Screening, for men, women, and teenagers through the CRT diagnostic machine, which also identifies inflammatory breast cancer (IBC), a triple negative. Because strokes kill twice as many women as breast cancer, my nonprofit also performs Free Beauty Shop Stroke Screening, as well as a quick three-minute Cardiovascular and Autonomic Nervous System Screening, using the FDA-approved medical device Max Pulse. I am a published author of an audiobook, "Written Before I was Born," which garnered me the recipient of the 2019 HerStory Award from the International Women's Federation for World Peace USA, where I serve as an ambassador. My prayers for all who read this are for an abundance of healing, love, kindness, and success on your personal, magical, magnificent journey of forgiveness and freedom.

Do not judge, and you will not be judged.
Do not condemn, and you will not be condemned.
Forgive, and you will be forgiven.

– Luke 6:37

Jeannette LeHoullier

Forgiveness will set you Free

by Jeannette LeHoullier

The result of adding Forgiveness into the mix of my decisions regarding relationships and my professional life helped to replace despair with positive action and ultimate empowerment, which in turn put the situations I was facing into a more positive perspective. The decision to act on forgiveness was not a new concept for me at all. I understood the concept and had faced unimaginable circumstances and trauma in my life, enough to know that forgiving can be more for the benefit of the person who feels victimized, than the person doing the victimizing. If you cannot forgive, then you are paralyzed in the moment and unable to move forward. In my 67 years of being in the world, I have unfortunately experienced numerous severe emotional, physical, and financial pain. Suffering quietly was nothing new to me.

Abuse was a hidden secret in my family and had been part of my life for as long as I can remember. What happened in my life that gave me an opportunity to forgive, not once, but far too many times? I was molested by a close relative as a baby, and it continued until I moved out on my own at age 18, during my senior year of high school. This was a terrible travesty and has affected my choices and decisions to an extremely high degree. As many know, childhood molestation leaves scars, and is worsened when it is from someone a child naturally expects respect and honor from. His actions and choices to violate my trust damaged my psyche and influenced my mistrust of others, especially men. My innocence was stolen from me and was replaced with PTSD

(Post Traumatic Stress Disorder).

Because I am a survivor and no longer victimized by abuse and I have chosen not to stay in a "victim mode" of thinking, I have recovered to the best of my ability. With tools and resources like counseling, I have improved over time. Throughout all of my negative experiences, I have strived to make lemonade out of lemons. I have also learned techniques that assist me in getting out of my head and remunerating issues that are to my detriment. I have accepted the need to reframe my experience so that I can manage and keep a joyful bliss-based lifestyle that are in alignment with my choices. To my own amazement at times, my upbeat attitude and joyful choices, have affected others in positive ways as well.

I can remember back on a time not so long ago in my professional life where I waited 9 months to be hired by a government agency, thinking it would be a fantastic opportunity and worth the wait time. During the Covid pandemic crisis, I reasoned with myself that the position would help assure my future and increase my earning power while helping the government agency to design and implement a technology program for isolated senior citizens in the surrounding local communities. To my dismay, my first day on the new job was filled with startling discoveries that rocked me and it was then that I knew I had to invest in myself, my community, and my own brand. Even now as I think back on this day, it remains a powerful turning point of clarity or an "ah hah" moment in my life. As a result of that "ah hah" moment, I chose to strongly pivot and I made a specific decision, took action, and outlined boundaries for myself. I began designing a new business model, logos, name, imaging as well as color branding for my own business. Rather, I choose to step into healthiness and empowerment, despite the hurt of very unpleasant actions.

In my business world, I chose the diva name, JOYFUL DIVA. People have commented on how they really enjoy listening to me laugh. With that in mind, it gives me goals to strive for and accomplish goals for my healthy state of mind. These concepts are also grounding as an entrepreneur, mother, friend, and colleague.

If you are new to the concept of abuse and then forgiveness, there are many resources and tools available to help you understand that you will forgive and grow past the abuse, small or large. One source is the Wheel of Abuse that a has a list of several types of legitimate abuse. If you or someone close to you has suffered from sexual or physical abuse, know that in fact the trauma is very real, and the effects are felt for the rest of their lives. A common thread for those effected are limiting belief stories that can easily attract narcissism and for me it was my male partners and husbands. Each marriage ended badly, and I allowed myself to be damaged repeatedly in those adult relationships perpetuating the abuse cycle.

Here are the main types of Abuse in the Cycle:

> Emotional/Psychological/Verbal Abuse
> Social Abuse
> Sexual Abuse
> Religious Abuse
> Ritual Abuse
> Physical Abuse
> Technology Abuse
> Environmental Abuse
> Financial Abuse

The Wheel of Abuse is marked with elements like:

Coercion & Threats
Intimidation
Verbal Attacks
Isolation
Minimizing
Denying & Blaming
Using Loved Ones
Abusing Authority
Economic Control

The Wheel of Change is comprised of:

Maintenance
Relapse
Pre-Contemplation
Contemplation
Determination
Action
Maintenance
Exit

Abuse and forgiveness are personal to me. I have lived in a domestic violence shelter and then became the first graduate of Bethany women's shelter run by the Sisters of St. Joseph of Orange. I am honored to have served for 8 years on the Advisory Board of Directors of Bethany. After I graduated from the 6-month intensive residential program at Bethany, I then was offered additional wonderful opportunities to use my strengths learned. I became the Chief Executive Officer (CEO) of The HealthCare Foundation for Orange County – helping low-income families in Central Orange County, CA with responsible health related grant programs to hospitals and non-profit agencies. While writing on the subject of forgiveness in Love Your Haters, I am reminded of an article I posted 11 years ago on my blog, JEANNETTE'S JOY. I entitled the post "FORGIVING – Is It Worth Trying to Let Go? The article posted on Monday, February 14, 2011. This date was impactful to me as it was the date, I published my article and was also the third anniversary of my marriage to my former spouse, who I thought was my "soul mate." I wrote the post to address some of the issues in the marriage and in my life with the hope that my negative experience may help other woman have a more positive experience in life. As we all know life is not perfect, and we as humans are surely not perfect either. I am grateful for my ability to forgive and have taken my experiences and my ability to find forgiveness and I apply that to my professional as a Senior Tech Tutor and Coach. I encourage tech users to guard their own devices with stronger safety settings, think before you post. You can have a valuable experience with newer technology which opens a broader way to communicate. In today's fast-paced world we are bombarded with both opportunities and challenges by utilizing social media because it is a public format. It is revealing to whatever the effect a person's privacy settings provides or does not provide. My first article for our local newspapers, Menifee Buzz and Murrieta Buzz, was entitled "Senior Technology, Nothing to Fear, But Fear Itself." Writing for the newspapers provides an avenue to inform and educate seniors, their families, and other users about common-sense technology options. Based on my firsthand experiences, I have written many other articles related to senior technology as well as family caregiving of the elderly with memory loss.

I am grateful that I applied for that position with a government agency. This gave me an opportunity to help others by providing tablets and tutoring services to seniors helping them to bridge the gap of generational tech divide. This provides up to date tech access to a demographic of many isolated older people. My experience in providing laptop, smartphone, and tablet tech tutoring to seniors, made the enticing job palatable as well as furthering my mission and goal to help by "Assisting with Integrity, Compassion and Patience," which is my own business tag line. My first day on the job, I was required to read the policies and procedures manual as well as the departments policies. Standard Human Resources requirement. I was shocked when I read about their conflict-of-interest policy because I realized that I would be required to give up my own Tutoring and Administrative company that I had worked a total of 11 years to build. I immediately felt like I had not been informed prior to my employment – which took 9 months. After waiting for the hiring process during the Covid pandemic and all the delays during that 9-month period, not once was I informed that I would be required to make a choice to give up my own entrepreneur business versus work for the government agency. This sudden realization, during the first day on the job, brought about emotions of anger, confusion, and worry. As I was driving home that first evening, I realized the job was not panning out the way I had been thinking it would. I would not have the steady income during my retirement years that I had anticipated and honestly, counted on. My goal had been to find a revenue stream of income before I would lose spousal support and be strictly Social Security Retirement funded which would then put me further in the high-risk poverty level. Honestly, I was terrified of being homeless again, as had happened after my divorce of September 2016. Tears began to roll down my face as I drove to my home as I prayed and asked for God's leading and answers.

I am a goal-oriented person, so all my hard work creating an altruistic community opportunity to serve senior citizens seemed to fizzle out when I realized my work/income situation was about to figuratively blow up in smoke. Whether as an employee or as CEO of my own company, I still felt a bit threatened, and I also felt taken advantage of and this felt like abuse. My well laid out plans were falling apart minute by minute, or at least that is what it felt like to me. However, God showed me over the next 2 days that he did in fact have a plan for my life. I thought about the scripture about "Joy Cometh in the Morning ... "(Psalm 30:5), such an appropriate verse. After sleeping on the hiring vs. business issue and speaking to a trusted business mentor, I came up with a plan that would eliminate the conflict-of-interest issue with the agency, and also afford me an opportunity to continue with my business, continue with a long earned opportunity to launch within a few days on unique Women Owned and with only Women Vendor associates. It was an exciting twist opportunity on e-commerce, or as they called it, SHe-commerce. A platform and website called The W Marketplace. This is a fantastic storefront-based business concept to explore. I had been approved 3 months prior to the government agency hiring date and I completed the intensive 6-week training to participate in the SHe-Commerce program and won a spot on the brand-new shopping website for women owned business - with unique businesses by women for women.

You know, I must stop for a moment and give myself a pat on the back, which has been difficult for me, because I was taught to be modest and not braggadocios and to play small. I had earned a spot on the unique She- Commerce shopping site, completed all my requirements to participate in the launch and figured out a way to legally, ethically, morally and with all the integrity I stood for. I worked to save my employment opportunity with the government agency and to still be able to keep my business with a foundation of integrity and passion. The Lord gave me the idea to take my concept created 12 years prior and turn it into a new focused business for women as my target audience, whether young, baby boomer age, families of this group, or just women in general. I allowed myself to remove the pressure off myself, to legally comply to the government agency, who had offered me zero life security. I was able to pivot creating assurance that I would continue to be a CEO of my own entrepreneurial business. My blog, JEANNETTE'S JOY is comprised of articles, thoughts, Quotes, Ideas, Recipes, News, and Photos. This was created, designed, and launched by me solely back in 2010. With God's guidance and a lot of strong work on my part, the blog became the catalyst as well as the foundation for my new rebranded business. By rebranding and renaming my business venture, I also became realigned with my life purpose to minister to women. The articles I have written over the last 12 years have allowed me to explore whether my ideas would be of interest to potential readers. It also set the foundation for becoming the author I had always thought I should be. Each one of us must always stay true to ourselves no matter what happens in our lives. We must not allow abuse, pain, hardship to take away our JOY, our PASSIONS, and our SAFETY.

I would encourage readers to reframe the loss or hurt that put them in a position to want to forgive or consider forgiving and allow the act of forgiveness to be a stronger solution over letting all the hurt turn into depression, low self-esteem, lack of motivation and/or numerous other negative emotions. Here are a few thoughts to take away as self-care and self-help solutions:

- Life is Messy ... "Make Lemonade Out of Lemons!"

- "Letting Go" often results in becoming lighter and brighter.

- "Forgiving Isn't for Sissies!" It takes an extraordinarily strong person to forgive when the

- harmful person does not take responsibility for the damage.

- Think of changes you will be making as a steppingstone to a brighter and happier life.

- When you think of the task of change and forgiving for your own self-preservation, please consider that it is like the Roses in my Garden – needing change or a process called "dead heading," which I learned from my wonderful Grandma "Amazing" Grace. Taking off the dead flower head of the rose will give the plant a stronger opportunity to have more blossoms – which brings a whole lot of JOY in life.

- The analogy of the rose represents change, death, rebuilding, with positive results obtained by your effort.

- You can live with DISCOMBOBULATED JOY by accepting the chaos and reframing it into something happier and manageable.

Giving Back – or giving to others – helps to take your thoughts off your own troubles and multiplies happiness for both you as a giver and to the receiver of your efforts. JOY, JOY, JOY!

May you all revel in the power of forgiveness and keep moving your life forward. For all that is secret will eventually be brought into the open, and everything that is concealed will be brought to light and made known to all - Luke 12:3. I look forward to serving my community and being a beacon on light that shines for all to see. We are better and stronger together; forgiveness will set you free.

Mayra Lewis

4,351 Miles Away

by Mayra Lewis

I moved to the United States from Peru in 2019, when I was 19 years old. I moved in with a cousin that I've only met twice in my life. You must be thinking, why did I make the decision to leave everything and everyone behind?

My biological father left us when I was just a baby; however, my mom had a boyfriend that I called dad. He treated me as his own and I love him a lot for it. He taught me so much and I feel I wouldn't be the woman I am today without him. At some point when I was younger, I felt resentment against my biological dad and his new family. Like any kid, I felt left out, and I wondered why we had to struggle with money all the time while they had so much? Why was it that he couldn't give me as much as he gave his other kids? I just couldn't understand how you can live knowing that your daughter went to bed without eating that night or that she was in the hospital with no money for medicine. That said, my mom, grandma and dad never let that resentment in my heart grow. They always told me that love was strong in the house and that whatever struggles we were going through, we could figure it out. We always did. Several times they didn't have enough money for groceries or basic necessities, and that made them ask for loans, which resulted in a lot of debt. As they said, love was strong, and that was all that mattered.

During my childhood, I had to be the perfect child. I couldn't go back home with a note from my teacher or a B, because I would get yelled at, grounded and sometimes spanked by my mother. It didn't matter how old I was or how good I was trying to be, I never had a chance to make any mistakes. I was always criticized for my weight and looks, with no chance to think for myself. I always wanted to do what was going to make my mom happy, and obviously that led me to a lot of pain. The last time I remember her hitting me was when I was 13 years old. Did I deserve it? Probably not, but that was her way of correcting me and teaching me things. She was also very strict with me, always checking where I was, reading through my phone and always listening to my conversations on the phone just in case I would say something she didn't like. I had to be the perfect daughter and as I grew it became harder and harder.

Growing up in a strict household led to a lot of lying and hiding stuff just to be who they wanted me to be. I couldn't go out with friends as often as others - no sleepovers, no boyfriends, essentially no social life, which led me to be bullied for several years. I became really good at deleting texts and talking in code words, everything so my mom wouldn't be on top of me all the time. High school was not fun for me and on top of that, at the time, I didn't know I was going through a personality disorder, which made things way more difficult: It led me to make bad decisions and that's when a lot of the rumors people made about me became true. In my mind I thought "Well, if they already have that perception of me, why not give them a reason to talk?" As you can imagine, I was wrong. Giving them a 'reason to talk' was, by far, my worst decision. Going to places where I shouldn't, running away from home just to get out of the toxic treatments or doing inappropriate things at school made me end up with no real friends. I ended up with an awful reputation and with my parents being disappointed in me. So, I decided to change and leave. In my senior year I switched high schools to where my mom was teaching at, it was a good choice. I made a couple of friends, and I had a great time, I even ended up third in my graduating class! Everything was going better, and I was finally recovering from the ghosts of my past... and then my parents got divorced.

You have to understand that I've always been 'daddy's little girl', even though he wasn't my dad biologically, he always loved me more than anything, just as I loved him. As a result, when they divorced, I got really depressed. I couldn't see my future without my dad, especially since he had a new family. I thought the story from my childhood was going to repeat, but I had to keep moving, no matter how much I missed him. I remember this happened right when I was about to go to college. It was 2018 and I was 18 years old, fresh out of high school. I was full of dreams about the future but at the same time, terrified. Because of my good grades, I was accepted into two of the most prestigious universities in my natural country. In March of 2018, I started my journey at the University of Lima and decided not to make the same mistakes. Full of hope, we managed to pay for one year of college. According to the University, my family was too poor to afford to pay for it, but too rich to be helped by any scholarship. Student loans are not a thing in my country and my dad had just left us, along with his financial help. With my mom's salary as a teacher, it was impossible to maintain a household and pay for college, so I had to drop out. So I had to start working, first as a party host for kids at a restaurant and then at a retail store. My salary was 930 soles, which for reference, is about $243. I was making that every month. I saw my dreams crushed; it was going to be impossible for me to go to college. I didn't have any money for anything and felt hopeless. My relationship with my dad was damaged because I said things I shouldn't have, which was influenced by my mom's resentment towards him. I didn't have many friends to rely on and the relationship with my mom was in recovery for what I did in previous years. What was I supposed to do?

That's when I thought about starting over. Somewhere where no one knew me, where I had a blank page to start a new story. One of my distant cousins moved to the U.S. a long time ago, so I contacted her and asked if I could move in with her until I got everything figured out and she said yes. We talked to my mom about it, and she agreed to it, so in September of 2019 I entered the U.S. through the airport in Houston Texas, leaving everything and everyone behind. Once again, I was full of hopes and dreams about the future and decided to be better, every single day and not make the same mistakes.

Within a couple of months of moving here, I ran out of the pills I take for my depression and my personality disorder, so I started having panic attacks and I felt very homesick. I had a job, but it was kind of hard for me to make new friends, so I felt really lonely. That's when I decided to try online dating, and that's how I met Brendan, my husband. We were married in 2022, and I think finding each other was the best thing that has ever happened to me.

Being in a different country, especially where the language is different and you don't look the same as others, made me feel less than the rest. Don't get me wrong, I was really happy to have a new beginning, but I felt like I wasn't enough. All of those thoughts went away when I met him. I trusted him enough that I could tell him about my past and he did not judge me. He made me believe that I could do anything that I set my mind to, he made me gain the trust in myself that I had lost. Everything finally started to take shape in my life.

I can confidently say that I've grown a lot since I moved here. I've been working on my goals and achieving so much; I was promoted really fast in the jobs I had and I'm always looking forward to being better and giving back to the community that received me with open arms. With Milvet I've been able to do that. Milvet is a non-profit that helps service members and veterans in Southern California. I'm a member of the Board of Directors and I love volunteering with them. We have an amazing team led by a wonderful CEO that I see as a mentor and aspire to be as empowered as her one day. In these two years with them I've attended many events and helped and met tons of people. Through them I became part of the GSFE (Global Society for Female Entrepreneurs), where I get to know amazing people and their stories.

Do you know what's great about hitting rock bottom? That you can only go up from there. And that's where I'm going! This is just the start of my self-discovering journey. I still want to finish college and become a bioengineer to help as many people as I possibly can, combining that with reaching more people through Milvet and being able to help them as well. I don't want to look back and say, "It could have been me", I want to live everyday like it was the last, sharing what I learned and spreading love.

I have finally come to terms with my past. I wouldn't be who I am today if I wouldn't have gone through it. I am thankful for the people I have in my life and for the ones that were just passengers. I have finally come to the realization that I am the one who tells my story, not anyone else, I'm the writer of my own life and you should be too. Don't listen to what others say, don't pay attention to rumors or whatever they say about you, you are the only one who knows your truth and you should be proud of it. Be proud of your past and your present, be proud of the scars in your life and always look forward to your future. There is no limit for what you can do. No matter how deep down you are, there's always a way to go up, to leave everything behind and start over. Step in my shoes for a second - I have traveled 4,351 miles away from my old life, left everyone behind and finally put myself first. I had to come all the way across the continent to find myself, find love and finally change my life, and I am certain that this is not the end. I'm still growing and working hard for what I want, setting goals, making mistakes, but always with my chin up, trying to be better every day.

Debbie Love

From Powerless to Empowered to Powerful

by Debbie Love

At a very young age I learned the value of a hug and how it can make you feel. A hug can make you feel safe, supported, and loved; it can also feel cold and uncomfortable.

My parents couldn't have been more different, and their hugs were much like their personalities. On my father's side, the 'Love' side, they'd pull you in and wrap you up tight in their arms. My Bubbie (grandmother) was the master and I loved being in her embrace. She was always happy when I was around like there was no one else she'd rather see. I miss her and her hugs; she showed me genuine love.

On the other side of the spectrum was my mother whose hug was stiff and indifferent. She was cold, rarely happy and difficult to please. She was more concerned about what others thought about this or that. When I think back, I'm not sure how well I really knew her. We weren't close and we had little in common.

I grew up in a suburb of Birmingham, Alabama (known as Mountain Brook) the youngest of four children. I had two brothers and a sister. In order of appearance, 1st Michael, 2nd Cindy, 3rd Gary and 4th is when I came on the scene. By the time I came along, my mother was worn out and any desire she had for raising kids had long passed.

In time I learned that they didn't plan to have a fourth kid; the first three were enough for mom. Lo and behold, less than a year after Gary was born, she was pregnant with me. I was not spared the knowledge that I was an accident which became a family joke.

The only rule in the house covered everything ... "DO WHAT YOU ARE TOLD." In all reality, this rule applied almost exclusively to Cindy and me. Tasks were optional for the boys but mandatory for the girls. Any 'ask' that came in the form of a question, wasn't a question at all. For example, "Debbie, would you please sweep and mop the kitchen floor?" While phrased as a question, it wasn't.

I was a good kid. One thing you learn when you're the youngest is what not to do. While I didn't cause problems or get into trouble, I was an enormous frustration and, in time, a disappointment to my parents.

The frustration and disappointment were because I didn't like to do the things other girls did. I enjoyed playing sports, climbing trees and getting dirty. I liked hanging out with my brother Gary and playing outside, riding bikes, playing catch, throwing a frisbee, or playing basketball until after dark. I wasn't a typical girl, who didn't sit well with my parents. I can still hear my mother say, "No boy wants to be beaten by a girl" or "Would you stop beating the boys?" or "All you do is show off!" I would hear this thing about showing off repeatedly. Fact is, I never showed off, it just happened to be the one and only thing that came naturally to me. I was quick and had good instincts. I won lots of trophies, yet my parents never came to watch me in any sports I played. Gary's games and Cindy's recitals were a family affair.

My mother would have preferred if I was more like Cindy who took ballet and wore Bobbie Brooks clothes. Mom loved shopping with Cindy but when I needed clothes, it never went well. Shopping was hell for me. I didn't care about clothes, I just wanted to be comfortable. She wanted me in more feminine clothes, flowery and pink. I didn't just hate the clothes, anything I got had to be altered so much that in the end nothing fit right. I was short and chunky, meaning I was overweight but not necessarily 'fat.' I was built like a 'Love,' like my father, short and muscular. To offer some perspective, in Juniors I was a size 13-15. When it came to clothes, all I ever asked for was cut off blue jeans.

I was eight the first time I was summoned into the bedroom by my father. I had just gotten home from a basketball game when I heard him calling for me. I figured mom needed help with her zipper again. When I walked into the room, I asked "Where's mom?" He didn't answer. He told me to lie down on the bed and when I asked "Why?," he gave a look that said, 'don't question your father.'

I didn't know what was happening and I wasn't allowed to ask. I did what I was told without question as I had been taught to do.

I was sad and had this strange secret. Was this wrong? Do all dads do this? This practice would go on for years.

When my breasts began to develop, they were extremely tender and hurt all the time. So, of course, dad started something new to exploit my new blossoming bosom. He was more eager to hug me tight and when he did, he'd move me from side to side so my breasts rubbed against his chest. Oh God this hurt! Again, there was no saying NO! Avoiding him was impossible. He did it to Cindy too though she was never willing to talk.

Sometime later, dad started a new 'thing' that he'd do to us. Any time one of us passed him in the hallway or anywhere else when no one was around, we had to let him pinch our nipples. We had to stop in front of him and offer up a breast nipple for him to pinch. If Cindy and I were walking together, he'd get twofer. When he'd spot one of us, he'd position his thumb and index finger as pinchers in a way of letting us know what was coming (and who had the power). It was humiliating. We endured this until we were each old enough to move out.

I don't recall when, but I started wetting the bed several times a week. This first time it happened, I woke mom and quickly learned never to do that again. From then on it fell on Cindy who would help me. I hated waking her, so I tried to stay up at night to avoid an accident. In the end I developed insomnia which I have suffered with ever since.

Before the bedwetting began, I'd spend most Saturday nights at my cousin's house. It was to escape my dad though nobody knew it. I was there so often that my uncle started asking "Don't you have a home?" I don't think he minded me being there, but I was there a lot more often. When I began wetting the bed, spending the night out stopped.

We lived in a great neighborhood with lots of kids. We'd play kickball, baseball, touch football, it didn't matter. We were playing hide and seek one day when an older boy ('Joey') from up the street wanted to play. I didn't know him well except that he had a red Schwinn ten-speed racing bike which I thought was cool. Joey had never played with us before, he was much older, and certainly too old for hide and seek. The game continued and when the counting started, everybody darted in different directions to find a place to hide. Joey grabbed my hand wanting me to come with him. He took me into the basement of his house to the far end where there was a small closet that held the furnace. He told me to lie down on the cold floor and began kissing and touching me. 'Wait - no - stop!' didn't deter him even a little. I wanted out and I tried to get up, but he held me down. I was totally powerless in the furnace room in the basement of a house I had never been in and with an older boy I hardly knew. I don't know how long I was in that basement, but weird details have stayed with me to this day, –the cold floor, and the smell of the furnace, his clothes and even his breath. It has never gone away. That was over 50 years ago.

I knew what he did was wrong, but I never said anything to anyone. And if I did tell, what was I going to say, 'Hey dad, Joey, did everything like you, except he kissed me too and made me touch his...

A lot of girls have these secrets, sexual secrets. Encounters such as what I experienced often stay with the victim for the rest of her life.

I'm sure boys like Joey never give it a second thought. Parents must do a better job of telling their daughters what some boys might try to do to them and what to do if they try. At the same time, conversations must be had with boys about the word NO and when they hear it, STOP. Most girls are afraid to say anything because they fear being blamed for causing it or accused of making it up, like I was.

Then this came out of left field - which blew me away. For my next birthday, I was completely flabbergasted with my parents' gift for me was a red Schwinn ten speed racing bike - they bought from Joey.

When I was about twelve or so, my mom was spending most of her time in bed and her moods were erratic. She was constantly taking medications, most of which were over the counter meds.

Then one day men in white coats came to the house and took mom away. It was shocking and difficult mom didn't know what was happening and dad said nothing to her; we all just watched it happen. After they left, dad said she'd be away for a while until she gets better. I didn't know she was sick; it was the way mom always was. Nothing was ever explained to me. I don't recall how long she was gone but I know while she was away, dad had complete access to me.

I was fifteen when I had my first real date. He came to the door and picked me up. Interestingly, I recall nothing about the date itself, not what we did or if we had dinner, nothing. I only remember the end when he walked me to the door and dad was waiting. When the door opened, dad said to my date, [and this is a direct quote] "So, did ya get any?"

I won my last trophy at age 24. I was at the community center with my brother when I met this guy from New York who decided to sign me up for a weight-lifting competition that was being held that day. I said 'NO, I don't lift weights', but he did it anyway. I knew the other girls who were competing had trained a long time for this event plus this was not something I would have signed up for especially because of my parents. In the end, I won the competition. This wasn't good news. After winning, someone from a wrestling magazine wanted to photograph me. They oiled me up to take the photo. Lord, I knew this was bad. The NY guy who had signed me up was excited and couldn't wait to meet my parents and tell them about my victory. I told the guy that I had no intention of telling them. When we got to the house, the guy wouldn't shut up about the competition and how I won and even showed them the trophy. Each word he spoke was digging a hole even deeper for me and I knew what my parents' reaction would be. Yep, they said these exact words, "So, you're going to scare off another one?"

I didn't like this guy; he was pushy and didn't listen when I said NO to the competition and NO to telling my parents about it. But he said we were getting married and when. I did–for 30 years. Finally, I got a divorce. It took all 30 years to gather the courage.

The moral of my story is when an authority figure or father molests his daughter at such a young age, she just might think that she has to let boys do things she may not want. She doesn't think saying "NO" is an option. Remember, I was told by my father that he was getting me ready for what boys would do to me. Because nobody else was saying anything about the topic, I had no other information.

This happened to me throughout my childhood and as an adult. It's only in the last few years that I gained confidence and strength to feel empowered. I am now literally a powerful woman because I have trained to be powerful, not because I was raised that way.

Now I teach young women to know what some boys do and what to do if they continue to try after you say NO.

#ISAIDNO

#grabtwistpull

Susie Mierzwik

Smack!!! I couldn't believe he just hit me!

by Susie Mierzwik

It was 1984, and I had just returned home after attending my best friend's wedding in New York. I was tired from my long flight, starving and anxious to reconnect. I wanted to share the details of the wedding and tell him about my first kid- free weekend. My husband was home watching our two small daughters. This was the first and only time I had been away from them. Always before, my husband "Bill" was gone doing his airline/Navy reserve careers while I held down the fort at home, with our children and my career. His re-entry to the home front was often tense and, it took a few days after his return to restore equilibrium. Today, something was off. He was pacing the floor of the living room and we started to argue about the state of our home. Sure, we had argued on his return home many times in the past. But this was MY first return home. I felt tense, something didn't feel quite right...

Then, as we were arguing, out of nowhere, I felt a hard slap!! I had a vague out of body experience as I noted the pile of dirty dishes in the sink. I could smell the garbage can which my nose told me hadn't been dumped all weekend. Was that the sound of my daughter crying in her bedroom? I struggled to make sense of this homecoming.

My cheek felt the hot flush and tears sprang to my eyes.   I had never been struck in the face before. When I recovered enough to realize what happened, I called the local police. His physical assault stunned me. Where had this come from? Is this the man who had promised to cherish me, in front of our parents a few years ago?

I couldn't believe this was my spouse, the father of my two precious babies. Why was this happening? What did I do to deserve this? I was exhausted from my long flight home, and I was scared. Who could I call for help or support? I had no one. The only thing I could think of was to calm him down. We had often argued before, but where did this assault come from?

Sensing his aggression, I felt like I did as a small girl. Whenever my mom was mad, I had to apologize to her. I never remember doing anything bad. Yet I was punished and had to say I was sorry again till she calmed down. This was the cycle I was accustomed to. When someone big and powerful got angry, I just closed up, put on a blank face, showed no emotion, and it would eventually stop. My adult daughters remember this incident happening so long ago, Although I was ignorant of the emotional consequences of this abuse at the time. I later learned that this had severe repercussions on them. This situation which they had observed, was frozen in their memories from long ago.

The fact that this was abusive behavior, didn't register with me. I just thought he was mad. Like many women who suffer from physical or emotional abuse, my feelings were mostly numb. I told myself that he was just angry; I told myself it was just about me. I had no clue that I was perpetuating a generational pattern of abuse that my own mom had suffered. She was oppressed as a young girl and closed emotionally. I am sure she did not realize that she was modeling the lack of nurturing she received which was handed down to me.

In 1997 I was sitting on our backyard patio by the pool in our spacious six-bedroom home. It was income tax season, and I had a side gig preparing income taxes for clients alongside my full-time career as a kindergarten teacher. I nearly fell off my chair when he handed me the divorce papers.

I had come out to the patio after work, with a cool glass of lemonade when "Bill" invited me to sit down. The hair raised on the back of my neck. In hyper clarity I smelled the lilacs blooming along the blue swimming pool. The warm breeze met the sweat that dripped down my back. What was I hearing? Divorce??? That was something that happened to "those other people". I was a good wife, wasn't I? We lived in the good part of a big suburban city. We both had careers and paid our bills on time? Divorce?? I couldn't even imagine being divorced!!

He said he wanted a TRIAL separation, and we would go to therapy; but he only went once, and claimed the problems were all mine. There had been other regular arguments when he returned from being on the road. Being apart a great deal of our time was a very challenging factor in our marriage. The balance of power shifted every time he crossed the threshold. He didn't understand the stress I felt dealing with the kids, our huge home, and our gigantic yard. He wanted to be Santa Claus, or a returning hero. Instead, he sometimes came home to broken appliances, discipline problems, and my loneliness. He later confessed that he had been seeing another woman while he was gone. Our daughters were aware of his affairs; they had even made email contact with one of his girlfriends. They carried this burden long before I was ever told of it. Another subsequent discovery during this time was that he brought me home an STD from which I suffered from for many years. This condition itself added another whole layer of physical and emotional grief to my experience.

I felt I had no choice but to accept the whole situation I was given. I remembered my vows said, "Till death do you part." It didn't occur to me that I could change what was happening to me or my circumstances.

Many years later after my divorce, I learned that his physical and emotional abuse caused damage on our daughters. My heart is crushed now knowing how his behavior caused them to suffer. They had no one to tell. Not even me!! They lived in a home where they never felt safe. They recently shared with me that they had wished we would get divorced so this situation would stop. They had to grow up too soon because their parents didn't provide a nurturing, safe environment.

It was only after the divorce, through therapy and divorce recovery, that I could see through my blinders. During my marriage, I never really felt anything deep. I thought that living meant just making the best of whatever you got and accepting your circumstances. I learned too late that the emotional environment children experience when they are little, has a critical effect on their self-esteem, confidence, and expectations for their whole life. So many realizations. So many lessons learned too late.

Dawn started to break on my dark days after about six months after the "trial separation." I had been attending therapy weekly to deal with the depression and confusion that accompanied my divorce. I remember driving to work in tears, praying that God would help me get through the day. I clung to the hope that we would reconcile, though that seems unrealistic looking back, because he only attended counseling once and said all the problems were mine!!

At this point a door clicked open in my heart, and I walked through into my future. I realized my old life was gone and I needed to create my new life.

Through a program called "Divorce Recovery", I learned about Boundaries. I discovered that it was not my job to make other people happy at the expense of my own heart and soul. I had been raised to keep my mom happy, and to be sure my own feelings were buried inside. I thought taking care of the feelings of others was my job, even if it did not serve me. The windows of my mind, heart and soul were opening! They were being washed clean through my tears.

Through Divorce Recovery I started to get in touch with my pain from decades of sadness in my childhood, as well as uncovering my own unmet needs in my marriage. Journaling allowed me to record my mixed-up feelings, even when I couldn't make sense of it all.

Weekly therapy provided the support I needed since I had no one else to share this burden. Regular Bible study was another source of comfort, encouragement and sisterhood. Having fellow Christian women hold me up in group prayer each week was my lifeline.

I started to do volunteer work as well. It was healing when I could still reach out and help others.

Physical activity was a great outlet. I joined a biking and hiking group. I worked out at the gym and took yoga classes. I eventually started to attend Christian singles dances with other friends.

Through all this emotional and physical work, I started to forgive my ex-husband. I saw how his emotional shortcomings and my own lack of emotional upbringing had created the perfect storm for our problems. I continued counseling which deepened my understanding of how the psychological climate I grew up in had a generational pattern. It stretched all the way back to my Dziadzia's (grandfather) traumatic youth in Poland when he had to escape his war-torn country to emigrate to America.

My Mom 's childhood had been emotionally abusive as well. She could never express herself or her emotions. She passed this unhealthy pattern down to me.

My ex-husband told me that he was physically mistreated as a child also which made him run away during elementary school. With so much unexpressed sadness, grief, and anger, our past experiences created the breeding ground for marital problems.

When I think about the additional strains created by my marriage to a pilot, I am amazed that our marriage lasted twenty-four years.

Several years after my divorce, I realized how my detachment had affected my daughters. I made sure they went to therapy to heal from their troubled childhood. One of them became a therapist herself, to help her clients to heal their own wounds. All of us have worked very hard to nurture our damaged hearts. I can see the change that has happened when I witness the gentleness and mindfulness in which my grandbaby is being raised. She is encouraged to express her feelings and emotions. This was something that had never been possible for me or my predecessors. I didn't even realize little people had feelings until I see how my daughter carefully helps her little child to express herself. Though it takes work and mindfulness in her job as a young mother, I witness the unfolding of a precious free spirit who is not being held down or silenced.

Through years of pain, prayer, forgiveness, learning, evolving, tears, and self-scrutiny, I have reached joy. During this journey I have come to practice thankfulness. This ancient practice still renews us. No matter how shattered we may feel in the moment, we can still find something to be thankful about. I knew the Lord was with me on my journey and writing down my list of blessings reminds me to keep going. There is a treasure to be found during our brokenness. If we look for something good, we will find it.

Susie Mierzwik

Lifewave
Live Long... Live Well...Live Younger
kinderkat9@gmail.com
9097093075
www.linkedin.com/susiemierzwik/
www.facebook.com/susan.mierzwik/

Dr. Robbie Motter

You Can Change Your Negative Thoughts to Positive Thoughts!

by Dr. Robbie Motter

Many years ago, when my doctor told me I had breast cancer you can imagine how at that moment my mindset went to stress mode. Later, we hugged, and I knew that whatever had to be done, I needed to do. So, I immediately shifted my mindset and thought about how lucky I was to be the mother of three wonderful children and grandmother to four beautiful youth. I thanked God for his love and the wonderful journey I get to go on every day. Suddenly having those beautiful instant thoughts made me smile and know all would be okay. I said to my doctor "schedule the surgery let's get rid of this cancer." That is exactly what was done. I knew all would be okay and in fact, two days after I had my left breast removed, I ran a board meeting. I was the President at that time for a Women's Club in my town and I keep my commitments.

You know it really starts with us. Do we really take time for things that bring us joy or are we always so busy helping others that we forget what we need as well?

I performed that way, but after the cancer I learned to be so grateful for each day that I am given. Each night before I close my eyes, I take time to reflect on the good things that happened that day no matter how small or how big. I find that as I think of those things, some of the things that did not go as well just disappear. It is amazing how such a small task keeps me always in a positive mindset.

I always remember something I heard years ago. BE YOU, DO YOU, LOVE YOU, and do what is FOR YOU!

It sounds so simple, but it seems that we as women constantly put ourselves on the back burner. So, I think if this is happening for you that you need to take time and ask yourself "why?" Once you know the WHY then it is so much easier to do for YOU first.

It's important to know that YOUR soul will never be solely nourished by anyone but YOUR own self. These words are so true and yet we constantly forget to do just that.

During the several years of Covid19, many were so blinded by it all because of so many unanswered questions that we found ourselves lost, depressed, some even without jobs, and even scared. I remember my first two days, I was getting into a bad funk, I was watching too much television no interest in dressing, putting on makeup or even being positive, which is not like me, and I did not like myself those two days. I knew I needed to go within and look at who I was and how I should be out there serving others. So, I said to myself "self this is not you, and how can you inspire and empower others when you are down." The next day I got up, got dressed, and put makeup on. I watched no television instead I listened to great upbeat music and my life came back to the Robbie I was prior to hearing about Covid19. I was again able to serve.

When it was time to get my Covid Shots, I thought of me and felt I had a great chance of keeping myself healthy and if I did get Covid, perhaps I would not have to end up in the Hospital. I also thought it would make me safe around others, so that was my mindset on getting them and I am still happy with my decision.

At that time, I looked at how my nonprofit Global Society for

Female Entrepreneurs (GSFE) a 501 (c)(3) could serve others. We had been having local live network monthly meetings. When covid hit that stopped. We looked at what we could do, and we pivoted to add Zoom monthly meetings instead to serve our members. So, we started adding Zoom which was a word that many did not even know what it was, yet alone know how to use it. Because we love serving and we kept a positive attitude we knew this was what we were meant to do.

We don't compete, we complete with others in our work, so we found some members in our network that had knowledge on Zoom. They taught us and this opened so many doors for us. Our membership grew and each day we also grew in knowledge that going back to self, made us feel great. We believed in ourselves and could take the journey to step out no matter what. Because we are now global, we have grown in membership and every month we get new members from all over the world. We have women from seventeen states that are members, and we have international networks as well. As of this writing, we have twenty (GSFE) nonprofit networks. Some that meet live again but many on Zoom. It has allowed our members to form relationships with women in other states and other countries.

I always remember this: "When a Bald Eagle appears you are on notice to be courageous and stretch your limits. Do not take this status quo, but rather reach higher and become more than you believe you are capable of. Look at things for a new higher perspective. Be patient with the present and know that the future holds possibilities that you may not be able to see."

YOU are about ready to take flight!

We have all had to face much trauma and stress in our lives, but when things happen "Believe in YOU and know that this will pass and tomorrow will be a better day and believe me it always is."

Remember when you are writing the story of your life, don't let anyone else hold the pen! It's your story, and your story could change someone else's life.

Be true to YOU, as you are beautiful, talented and amazing just the way you are. Every day is an opportunity, so step out, and grab it.

Robbie Motter is the founder/CEO of the Global Society for Female Entrepreneurs (GSFE) a 501 (c)(3) nonprofit she formed in 2017. Prior to that she served women for over 29 years as the N.A.F.E global coordinator. Her passion is working with women to help them soar higher than even they imagined. She is also a Certified International Speaker, Award winning #1 US and International Author with her book "It's All About Showing Up and the Power is in the Asking." She has also been a contributing author in numerous other award-winning books.

Her websites are: globalsocietyforfemaleentrepreneurs.org and robbiemotter.com

She can be reached at rmotter@aol.com.

Lori Raupe

Faith, hope and love;
the greatest of these is love

by Lori Raupe

Did you grow up believing it was wrong to hate? When I think, *Love Our Haters*, my first thought, *Can I say hate? Who hates me? I hope no one hates me! YIKES!*

In this short chapter, I'll give you a way to have a more fulfilled life without hate. But, a disclaimer, I am a certified coach, not a therapist. Why is love greater than faith and hope, and mentioned more in my favorite book? Love is mentioned 542 times and hate only 86. I believe this is a great way to operate, love more, and hate less. Where does hate fit in? Hate is a strong word, and maybe you are like me, I wasn't allowed to say "hate" growing up.

Remembering back to one day in my teen years, I told my mom, "I HATE you!" Something I deeply regretted afterwards. We want to be judged on our best days, but some will judge us on our worst days. That was one of my worst days. Gratefully, Mom understood the PMS driven moment.

I don't think I have any haters, and I know I don't hate anyone. So why write a chapter in this book? I've seen this as a sticking point when people want success in their life. Often, they won't say they hate anyone, but... When we have "enemies," or "hate" people, honestly even dislike people, we are missing something so valuable in life. The value of our human experience as women, and an understanding of this powerful emotion. Because I have helped many people through coaching, I thought maybe this could help you.

Haters? Do you know anyone who hates you? Were you unfairly judged? I think the strong emotion of hate comes from judgment. I spent 25 years in prison. It shocks most people when I say it! I usually pause for a reaction...after people realize what I said they laugh, nervously. It's a cheeky joke, I was not an inmate, it was my career. My assignments took me all over California to most of the 33 prisons. During my career, I learned a lot about human behavior and specifically about judging people. In prison, it is survival to judge others and your surroundings; otherwise, you can come to great harm. Although I learned many things while working for the prison system, one lesson comes to mind when I think about *loving your haters.*

Over 20 years ago I had what the inmates called a "Cadillac" job, which was in risk management to reduce inmate lawsuits. I loved the job, the travel, the extra money I earned, and the work itself was very interesting.

California State Prison at Corcoran: they housed many notorious inmates. Sirhan Sirhan, who killed Robert F. Kennedy, mass murderer Charles Manson, and many others. I was there to interview Inmate Smith; he was escorted to a small room where I would interview him regarding his complaint. He was a "C" number, which meant that he had been in for a long time and likely a murderer or rapist. As he sat down, he looked angry and mean. I noticed many tattoos. He would be easy to *hate*, if I was the hating type.

Above his eyebrows were two words — a four-letter word beginning with "F" above his right eyebrow and "Y-O-U" above his left. I felt like he was swearing at me as he spoke. I never forgot those tattoos and how they made me feel that day.

Years later, it was just before Thanksgiving in 2015, I was the Community Resource Manager. A unique opportunity was offered by a non-profit organization to promote literacy. They supplied children's books to be read and recorded by the inmates. Volunteers would send the recording and the book to a child the inmate had designated to receive their Christmas gift. The wardens supported the program, and I loved being a part of it as I oversaw the details.

On the first morning, I was helping the inmates find the right books to read. As I looked at the long line of inmates, there he was again — Inmate Smith with the swearing tattoos. As he made it to the tables with books, I noticed he picked up a princess book. I thought to myself, "What a contrast!"

With the princess book in hand, I escorted him into an office so we could record him reading the book. It wasn't a challenging read, but he struggled much like a first grader. He was frustrated when he messed up and asked to start again. I could tell he wanted it to be perfect for his granddaughter. I saw his pain and frustration, just like it must have been when he was a boy. I had always wondered why someone would put a tattoo like that on their face, now I started to see the answer.

I saw the years of pain in his eyes as I encouraged him. He smiled and thanked me for my kindness. We both had tears in our eyes.

Wayne Dyer said, "When you judge another, you don't define them; you define yourself." His words caused me to start noticing when I was judging others. Maybe it is because of my age, but I look at things though a different sense these days.

Babies don't enter the world hating or wanting to die a bitter old person. Holding on to resentment, anger, and un-forgiveness is like taking poison and hoping another person will die, but we die inside instead. Forgiveness is more about our happiness than those we forgive. I know, it all sounds so good, but how do we forgive? How can we love those who have hurt us? How can we release resentment?

A coach challenged me to look for areas where I might have resentment. I am most grateful I've embarked on this journey of discovery. Through the approach I developed for myself, and now have taken countless clients though, I have seen an amazing transformation. In a nutshell, you become aware, articulate the circumstances, release, forgive. Of course, there is more to it, and I'll describe a part of the process below if you want to get started on a journey of healing for yourself.

Releasing the negative emotions has been described as, "A weight has been lifted," "I don't feel anger like I did," and "I feel more at peace with myself!" I see these breakthroughs regularly with my clients. My hope is this process can help you too.

As a coach, I have seen tremendous and meaningful results when taking clients through heart healing sessions and using the system, I developed to release resentment and forgive. Journaling adds a layer to the process and gives a way to remember and anchor your thoughts. Here is the process below:

1. Begin with awareness. Pick a quiet time to focus, ask yourself, *"Do I have any unresolved anger, resentment, or someone to forgive?"* If you are a person of faith, ask God to help you. Wait for the thoughts and make a list of everything that comes to mind, no more than 5 minutes. After that, pick one that stands out the most.

2. Write down the details, start with, "Who, what, when, why,

and how." Just write until you feel you have gotten it out and onto the paper. No more than 30 minutes total.

3. Write about how it could have been better, could the other person have done something differently? Could you? Reframing is powerful, use your imagination to write the details. Yes, you can rewrite the past with how you would have preferred the situation to have played out.

4. Consider why you might want to let it go. Then, write about it. Choosing a date to let it go works well for some of my clients.

5. Look inward for any way you may have been responsible for the situation, forgiving yourself may be a part of your process.

6. When you are ready and have poured your heart out onto the paper, let it go. Do what feels good to you, some like the symbolic gesture of taking your paper and ripping it up into tiny pieces. Some people burn it in a dish or the fireplace. (Warning: make sure it is safe.) If you think there may be more, do this over several days, even months.

7. Write about your feelings after the release of emotions.

When you journal keep these thoughts in mind:

- Separate people from the action(s). A single act doesn't define a person. Much like our circumstances don't define us. Certainly, what someone does may be wrong, but they are more than one event or act. If it is ongoing, even still, they are not what they do.

- Forgiving does not mean forgetting. We have memories, and we may need to move forward with caution in relationships to protect ourselves. Establish boundaries in your life. You may decide to remove toxic people from your life.

- There are always two sides to a story, sometimes we judge without knowing all the facts. Judgment isn't our burden to bear, but we often think it is.

- Ask yourself, can I "let it go?" Sometimes, we simply make the decision. Stop wasting energy on the negative and stop holding on to unnecessary anger. Where our focus goes, our energy flows, and the object grows. This is true of both positive and negative emotions.

- Remember, a person can only give what they have to give. If we lack love and understanding, we can't give it to others. If possible, give them the benefit of the doubt without adding any assumption.

Years ago, it was suggested that I write a letter to my step-grandfather who stole my innocence. I wrote about how he hurt me, and its effect on my life. You may want to write a letter, then burn it, tear it up, or save it as a reminder of your emotional growth. I do want to caution you about sending it, their reaction may not serve the purpose intended, and can be devastating to you, I don't recommend it for this reason.

What if the person you need to forgive is yourself, or you've hurt someone? Admit it, don't let pride get in the way, honestly life is too short. Let the person know you are sorry and accept your responsibility even if you didn't intentionally hurt them.

Learn from your mistakes. Be transparent; secrets can create shame. In the long run, you will be respected if you admit your mistakes, own them, and do your best not to make the same mistake again, but when mistakes happen more than once, look for the motives.

Don't beat yourself up, move on. The past is in the past, we don't get redo's. Tear off that rear-view mirror and stop looking back. Consider this, if you were given time to rethink the situation and have a redo, you might not have done the same thing. Give yourself grace.

When I have gone through this process, I have seen more people with a lens of love. It changes you from the inside out. Love becomes the predominate word for your life. What if we lived as if we were dying? Who would you ask to forgive you? Who would you forgive? Is it time? Why wait? This practice is life-changing, transformational. I am a better person because of it. Looking back, I've forgiven, and received forgiveness.

Like you, I've been hurt me and betrayed, and it wasn't always easy to release the emotions. Through "heart-healing," I discovered unresolved areas in my life where I "drank the poison." If you want to truly feel peace in your soul and have more joy, this is worth every minute. You deserve it!

Want additional information? Take the EQ (Emotional Quotient) Quiz, or schedule a consultation:

https://linktr.ee/LoriRaupe.

Lisa Ray

Haters are Gonna Hate
Use Your Haters to Fuel Your Success

by Lisa Ray

Everyone has haters, especially those aiming to achieve success in life and business. The experience of having a "hater" can start out early in life with the feelings of winning and losing. School yards are full of examples of those who notice your growth game and begin to angle with you, or against you. As you grow you find that some people just don't believe in your work or those that just outright disagree with your point of views for no apparent reason than a willingness to expand and grow their own views. The truth is we never really know what someone else is going through or their triggers. While having haters in your life brings negative energy into your life, these interactions actually offer a great benefit to your career. I work to create digital content and produce brands via marketing and media. I have learned to take on this topic "Haters are Gonna Hate, "by remembering these lessons I have learned along the way. I always try to make criticism my fuel and not my kryptonite. It is all about how you frame it in context. I try to take the negativity in and take it as a compliment. You're going to inspire envy as your star continues to rise, right? I have learned over the years that the second you take negative comments personally, you're losing.

Remember that really successful people don't have to put others down. Happy people don't waste their time saying negative things about others, why would they? Killing your haters with kindnesses, is a skill that will break down barriers. Be a shining light and live large so that others can see that it is possible. Often times, I take the opportunity to check in with myself. I've realized an important lesson: No matter what you do, people will always criticize your actions when they are personally triggered and when your plan or brand can offer solutions. Embrace the criticism. Uncomfortable moments are usually the sign that you are on the right track. Often in these moments, I try to ask myself if there is something I can be learning from this. If the criticism is a harsh attack, don't respond with another grenade. Listen to the criticism but don't give up. The best, most powerful advocates often start out as your toughest critics. Don't ignore critic's feedback. Listen to them and engage with them constructively. Getting you to feel defeated is a critics ultimate goal. Don't give up. Persistence, direct action, and passion are the key elements to your entrepreneurial endeavors. Above all, stick to your convictions. Keep striving with your own moral compass and integrity. Thoughtful research and conviction are the roots to confidence.

Below are 3 tips on How to Use Your Haters to Fuel your Success. If you are able to internalize the bigger picture and compartmentalize the feedback, you will fuel your success.

Here are my top 3 tips on How To Use Your Haters to Fuel Your Success!

Hater as we call them, are actually a blessing in disguise and can bring the love of your work back to you. In a world where everyone is posting daily, it gets harder and harder to find really loyal brands and their friends as you climb to the top of your ladder. Honestly, most people in your immediate circle are just too close to the mission, vision, or plan and don't want to hurt your feelings. So, all you will usually get is praise from them, and even when you want them to be honest, they'll most likely sugarcoat it when it comes to the truth. It is our job as entrepreneurs to diffuse and reuse this energy to fuel us on our journey to move our own life forward.

"When it comes to your haters, they are gonna hate."
- Lisa Ray

When it comes to your haters, they're fine with laying down all your flaws and weakness in your space. While they aren't right 100% of the time, it does give you a lot of good information on how you can improve yourself. Creating content that feels empowering can and will be challenging. Having clear vision and traveling forward in your own career and personal lanes of life are what makes you unique. When I am most triggered, I became hyper aware of this thought, **"what about this hateful comment that I am reading is triggering my internal response?"** In general, I scan and trace the feeling back to an outdated and limiting belief system. Thoughts would come to me often like, "You're not good enough therefore you don't deserve success, love, or respect as an entrepreneur." In many instances, I am the one who is set free in this very moment as this statement or limiting belief like a broken recording in my mind, no longer has a hold on me. That outdated song that began playing on school grounds, with abusive partners, or instances where your internal light was too bright for others, and you were asked to dim for another to shine bright. Standing in the moment and staying present is key.

1. **Awaken to the triggered feeling of an outdated storyline.** It was told to you, it can give you internal power to become aware and present and also to witness this knowing feeling that this is the old song, a hater's message, and this awareness will set you free. *"What you are is what you have been. What you'll be is what you do now - Buddha*

2. **Name it to Claim it and it will no longer have power over you.** Given the chance to see these negative interactions as a positive, create moments of gratitude and pride. Respecting your internal dialogue and only allowing in, what matters to you will turn what was once negative into the ultimate positive energy of moving you from being so scared of your own future and derailed by the judgement, and shame that kept you playing small. In the newfound space of knowing this is a limiting belief, tell yourself, I am moving my life forward and building a community of forward thinkers and spiritual leaders that have the knowledge that you are what you speak into being. I know it will help you as well. I believe that if you allow the perception and judgement of others to guide you in your own space, your judgement becomes jaded and untrue of your own storyline.

3. **Your Haters keep you grounded.** Having too much praise and flattery around you is not always the path to success and fortune. This can cloud your judgement and mind and you can forget where you came from or why you started at all. Similar to my first two points, if all you hear are good things about yourself, you will lose focus on your set goals. Ultimately, having people that don't like your ideas, beliefs, or outlooks reminds you that you're not the center of the universe and you still have a way to go. I pride myself on having in my tribe; family, friends, and a trusted circle that I have known my entire life. Some friendships of nearly 40 years. I have joy and peace with those I trust most in my immediate inner circle. I find that I live in a space where I am the student and then at times the teacher. The exchange of ideas is powerful. Allow yourself to be guided by new thoughts and practices that will deepen your skills and make you sharp in all meetings.

Collaboration, research, and communication are your superpowers. Channeling these elements into your work will give you the confidence to flip the page, scroll on by, or then ultimately help you to understand that your reader, coworker, or life partner has been triggered, not you, them. I have a dear friend who owns a brand on IG and their posts are about being open minded and leading with intentions, gratitude, and love. I have read her haters messages, "I feel as if you're speaking to me and targeting me." The brand says," if you feel that way, then maybe it was meant for you to hear today, and we are here to guide you." Kindness diffuses. Information hits us all differently depending on how we receive the messages. Change is difficult but certain and those with unseen triggers will respond in a negative way. As we have learned together, this is ultimately their issue, not yours dear one.

"In general, I can trace the feeling back to an outdated or limiting belief system. When your response is to be paralyzed by fear in the moment or frozen in your space, you have been triggered. Staying calm and having heightened awareness of this physical reaction will help you to name the feeling in the moment, staying present. This moment of realization is crucial to moving you back in a forward motion of flight. Haters cannot strategize because hate blinds you and makes you play small. The low-level energy makes you act irrationally, so actually, they're not really a threat. They cannot think long-term and cannot see a bigger picture."

"They are not as strong as you might think they are." - Lisa Ray

Your Haters are Gonna Hate and the interactions will challenge you. I have found that very few influencers and new businesses keep the course and that few are able to channel that energy into motivation to work harder instead of shying away and retreating. This ultimately changes the trajectory of the path of their own brands course. Remember this, successful people don't have to put others down and have full control. You are given a chance to either choose to see other's critical views of you as a way to bring you down, or an indirectly see what you may use as fuel to make you push harder.

Use the opportunity while experiencing the nay sayers, haters, non-believers and learn to navigate conduct and love those who love to hate. This may make you more appreciative of your own individuality and be a reminder to be grateful for how far you have come and the uniqueness, talent and fortune that you have. Their opinions only matter if they matter to you.

LYH

Kelly D. Smith

Fear Has No Hold On Me

by Kelly D. Smith

How do you love a person who has caused a lot of physical or emotional pain to you, either on a one-time event or on a repeated offense? Is unconditional love really possible? The Bible tells us that God has this kind of love for us. As humans, are we capable of unconditional love? For many parents, unconditional love for their child is possible. You may not like that your child stole a candy bar from the grocery store, but you still love them. You may not like that your child was dealing drugs on the school campus, but you still love them. You don't approve of the actions, but you never stop loving them. Can you love the stranger on the street, the homeless person on the corner? Possibly. Can you love the rapist, or child molester, the murderer sitting in the prison cell, or the drunk driver that barreled through the stop sign, hit your car and caused injury or death to a loved one? I feel that there are some people that are capable of this kind of unconditional love. There is also, I believe, not a love, per se, but a kind of forgiveness that releases you from bondage. Bondage from anger, bitterness, hatred, and self-loathing. Forgiveness is not for the offender, but for the victim/survivor.

How do you forgive the person who raped you? Maybe you were molested as a child, had a father who beat on you every time he came home from the bar. I don't know what you're dealing with, but I do know that a majority of people have some kind of baggage they are carrying around and just don't know how to set it down and move on. Some of us have fear that has developed in our lives due to the injury we acquired at the hands of someone else. We didn't ask for it or want it, but there it is, years later, still eating at us, still nagging at us in our minds. Maybe, we still cry or are still so full of anger or fear that it is affecting our health. We have high blood pressure: we can't sleep at night. Anxiety has become our middle name. How do we forgive, let go, and move on? For me, I found my healing through the Word of God and prayer. I want to share some key scriptures that helped me and hope that they will do the same for you.

As a young woman, barely out of my teens, I was raped at gun point. This event caused me to live many years in fear. Distrusting of men. I wanted this man to hurt as I had been hurt. To feel as I felt. Reading, studying, and praying the word of God healed my heart and mind. God's word changed my life. I went from a place of despair to a place a hope. A place of depression to a place of joy. I no longer let fear run my life, I have learned to move past it. Fear doesn't control me anymore. I'm not saying I don't have fear, I do, but I don't let it control me anymore.

Courage is not the absence of fear, but rather it is having fear, but still moving forward. I'll give you an example. My oldest daughter signed up to go on this tour in Switzerland to walk on the tallest suspended bridge in Europe. The bridge is 10,000 feet above the ground. My daughter told me, "Mom, I'm afraid, but I'm doing it anyways." And you know what? She did it. She has some of the most beautiful pictures and memories to last a lifetime. The confidence she has comes with the ability to conquer fear.

After the rape, I had to deal with fear. Fear of going out, fear of staying in, fear of being alone, fear of sleeping, fear of strangers. There were two scriptures that helped me immensely. I learned that I am never alone. The Bible says, "So do not fear, for I am with you; do not be dismayed, for I am your God. I will strengthen you and help you; I will uphold you with my righteous right hand." [Isaiah 41:10, NIV]. I also relied on this verse to help me, "For I am the LORD your God who takes hold of your right hand and says to you, Do not fear; I will help you." [Isaiah 41:13, NIV].

Once I conquer one fear, another one shows up and I can feel God saying, "Ok, you dealt with that one, no let's work on this one." Here is an example of how God is continuing to work on my fears. This incident happened to me recently. I don't know how to swim, so I am always nervous when I have to go over a bridge that is over water. The Richmond Bridge in Northern California, by Oakland and San Francisco, is a very tall and long bridge that crosses over the ocean. I have to cross it to get to Southern California. When I first started driving over the bridge my hands gripped the steering wheel so tight that my hands ached afterwards. I stared straight ahead, afraid to look off to the side to see the water. The more I drove it the more relaxed I became. I started to say to myself before getting on the bridge, "I got this." My hands didn't grip the wheel that tight anymore and I actually looked off to the side a little and saw the water.

My youngest daughter told her friend how I was afraid to drive on the bridge because I don't know how to swim. Her friend told her, "That's a very tall bridge, it doesn't matter if she doesn't know how to swim. The fall will kill her." Although this statement is true, I don't think that statement helped me.

Anyway, one of the last times I crossed over the bridge I got lost. I somehow ended up in the wrong freeway lane and found up on the wrong freeway. I didn't notice it for about an hour. The map app on my phone had me turn around and took me back through San Francisco. The app said to exit 19th street. I thought 19th street, it's taking me over the Golden Gate Bridge. Sure enough, I ended up driving on it. The Golden Gate Bridge is over the ocean of course and it is taller and longer than the Richmond Bridge. It was dusk by this time.

After I crossed over the G.G. Bridge, my phone app looped me around and took me over the Richmond Bridge, again. This time it was dark. I drove over the bridge in the dark! On the way back home, I decided that I had enough bridges and would stay on interstate 5. I thought that way I won't have to cross over the Richmond bridge again. Well, little did I know, that God was not finished with me and bridges, yet. This new way I chose to take home had bridges, and they were also over water. They are smaller than the G.G. bridge and the Richmond Bridge, but they are still over water and there are 4 or 5 of them. Two of the bridges are draw bridges. I have never crossed over a draw bridge before. Do you think I learned my lesson? I failed. I not only had to drive over all these bridges, (which included two draw bridges,) but I had to drive next to a large body of water. There were no barriers next to this lake. As I drove very close to this lake. I said out loud to myself, "Oh great, now if someone hits my car, my car is going in the water." I am sure that there are more bridges over water and more roads next to water in my future.

Another issue I had to deal with concerned how I viewed myself. My advice to you is for you to realize three things. 1: You need to understand that it was not your fault. 2: You are not to blame. 3: You need to start loving yourself again. I battled for years with loving myself. I felt ugly, not worthy of being loved. I lost my self-confidence and self-esteem. It was only through the word of God that I was able to overcome the emotional trauma of the rape. Start seeing yourself as God sees you. God says, "Since you are precious and honored in my sight, and because I love you . . ." [Isaiah 43:4, NIV]. Furthermore, start praising God for creating you. You are a unique, one-of-a-kind masterpiece. "I praise you because I am fearfully and wonderfully made; your works are wonderful; I know that full well." [Psalm 139:14, NIV].

I had trust issues that I needed to deal with. I didn't trust men, but this trust also went into other areas of my life, and I soon found myself not trusting anyone. They had to prove themselves to me first as trustworthy before I would open up to them and be close to them, either physically or emotionally. I learned to trust God, then I was able to learn to trust others. "When I am afraid, I put my trust in you." [Psalm 56:3, NIV].

The Lord commands us to forgive. "For if you forgive other people when they sin against you, your heavenly Father will also forgive you." [Matthew 6:14, NIV]. Many people are reluctant to forgive. They hold on to anger, which does nothing to the person who hurt them, but the person offended does continue to hurt. When you don't forgive, you become bitter, and bitterness turns to anger. No one wants to be around a bitter, angry person. Your friends and family stop calling and hanging around you because they don't like your bitter attitude. Attitudes are contagious. The best way to forgive someone is to pray for them. Pray that you are able to forgive them, pray that God blesses them. Yes, pray for them to be blessed. Let go and let God handle it. Don't be confused because you don't feel like you have forgiven. Remember, we walk by faith, not by feelings. Just keep praying that you forgive this person and one day your actions will match up to your words.

You can only be healed when you let go and stop living in the pain. Forgiveness does not mean you forget the incident. It doesn't mean you don't recall the details. It just means that you're not going to let what someone did or said to you control and dictate your life anymore. In the Bible, in the book of Genesis, chapter 32, we read the story of how Jacob wrestled all night long with God. He went face to face with God until morning. When God saw that Jacob wasn't giving up until he blessed him, God stopped. He gave Jacob a new name, Israel. "Then the man said", "Your name will no longer be Jacob, but Israel, because you have struggled with God and with humans and have overcome." [Genesis 32:28, NIV]. We also read that God touched Jacob's hip and from that moment on Jacob walked with a limp for the rest of his life. "When the man saw that he could not overpower him, he touched the socket of Jacob's hip so that his hip was wrenched as he wrestled with the man." [Genesis 32:25, NIV].

When we go through painful experiences, whether physical or emotional, sometimes we are left with a scar. It can be a physical scar that is seen and felt, or it can be a scar on the heart that is invisible to the eye, but nonetheless, a scar. A physical injury can leave us limping like Jacob or mean the loss of a leg and be left using a prosthetic leg but make no mistake that your healing hasn't happened. The scar, limp, etc. are just reminders that you are an overcomer. You had the victory, and this is just a reminder or a testimony of what you survived and overcame. "I have told you these things, so that in me you may have peace. In this world you will have trouble. But take heart! I have overcome the world." [John 16:33, NIV]. With God, we are overcomers. We not only are overcomers, but we are healed physically and emotionally. It's time to take off the invisible bandages, and accept your healing, even if you still have a scar or a limp. You are healed. "He heals the brokenhearted and binds up their wounds." [Psalm 147:3, NIV]. It's time to start thanking God for your healing and start living in the healing you have received.

Some people see instant healing and others are a work in progress, but that doesn't mean it isn't happening. I took many years to recover. God peeled away at me in layers, like an onion being peeled. He worked a little at a time in different areas of my life. One way to know you are emotionally healed is when you can talk about the event without crying, sweating, or shaking. The memories are still there, but they are not painful anymore. In other words, you remember, but you don't relive it. The infected wound has closed and is healed. A scar may remain, but all warriors have scars left behind from their battles. Remember to see yourself as a survivor, not a victim. You are a survivor.

Charmaine Summers

Forgiveness

by Charmaine Summers

When having moments of weakness and loneliness, counteract those feelings with strength and courage.

Keep going

Find reasons to achieve your goals and succeed

Keep going

Band together with people you can bond with and create an inner circle of achievers

There is a storm inside all of us

A desire to push ourselves harder

At the highest volume of winning

Inner-strength

Sharing without holding back

Exuding a unique beam of light that only you possess manifesting from your kindness and beauty inside and out

It is much like a race, you feel the energy the power the strength to cross the finish line

Some unknown force pushing you to that finish line

Focus

Prepare to win, to be strong, to plan for the right outcome

Asking yourself, what does it take ?

Again, remembering when you were younger and took a run around the High school track

What an exhilarating feeling! Running to cross the finish line. What a feeling! Wow you made it.

While running towards the finish line pushing yourself . . .finding your inner strength . . .your breathing heavy and grasping for air . . . there is a storm brewing inside to win and cross that finish line.

We have had this feeling of energy and desire to endure since we were young!

It's still there!

Having moments of weakness

counteracting as feelings of loneliness or depression .

Keep Going

Find your balance again

Strive for success !

One step at a time

Surround yourself with positive energy.

Prepare each day to win

Find your inner strength again

Find your beam inside, only you possess

Remember!!!

Find your Forgiveness

Then you will win once again

Forgiveness

Remember hurting so bad by the actions of a friend, you thought it was impossible to go on?

You did move on and how long did the sadness take up space in your mind, heart and soul?

Sometimes, too long!

Now we are much more mature, the pain of it all, should no longer consume your time and energy .

We must go to our highest level of forgiveness and know there is an ending of pain if we let it end in our heart of hearts. Only we possess the Power to end the hurt.

Find your finish line and run joyfully towards it . . . push to win!

Charmaine Summers

Run to the Finish Line!

Dr. Nephetina Serrano

The Greatest of These Is Love

by Dr. Nephetina Serrano

"But to you who are listening I say: Love your enemies, do good to those who hate you, bless those who curse you, and pray for those who mistreat you. If someone slaps you on one cheek, turn to them the other also. If someone takes your coat, do not withhold your shirt from them. Give to everyone who asks you, and if anyone takes what belongs to you, do not demand it back. Do to others as you would have them do to you. If you love those who love you, what credit is that to you? Even sinners love those who love them. And if you do good to those who are good to you, what credit is that to you? Even sinners do that. And if you lend to those from whom you expect repayment, what credit is that to you? Even sinners lend to sinners, expecting to be repaid in full. But love your enemies, do good to them, and lend to them without expecting to get anything back. Then your reward will be great, and you will be children of the Most High, because he is kind to the ungrateful and wicked. Be merciful, just as your Father is merciful." *Luke 6:27-36 NIV*

We are expected to make it our goal to love as our Heavenly Father loves. Loving our enemies doesn't mean allowing them to continue to hurt us. That would be a failure of loving ourselves as God loves us. We can do what is in our control to protect ourselves while trusting God to step in. God Commanded us to Love however, He never said, "we had to give them our heart. Our heart belongs to God and on the contrary God tells us to guard our hearts. Guarding our hearts means being wise and discerning in our lives. It means *protecting ourselves from all the things that would come to harm us.* Our heart is the most important leadership tool we have. It is your heart that matters most. It is not your experience, knowledge, or skills. *Michael Hyatt*

The reality is that we live in a world where men are only concerned about what's in it for them. Gone are the days that we are our brothers and sisters keeper. Matters of the heart, matter to God. When our heart is hurt God is saddened. I realize how much God loves me when I cry, I realized he is moved to action by my tears. I learned no matter what people do or say to try and break my spirit it will never work because God has created me to WIN and therefore, I can look to the hills and to the Lord for strength. You must first know who you are and whose you are. Our first point of overcoming is just that, knowing who you are. Knowing that you were born to win. You, yes you. We are more than conquerors. Secondly, know that you are created in the image and likeness of God and you were built to stand every test of time that comes your way. When there is purpose attached to you people will come for you and at you with all that they can to tear you down to discourage you and to destroy you. God says, **"A thousand may fall at your side, ten thousand at your right hand, but it will not come near you."** You will only observe with your eyes and see the punishment of the wicked. then no harm will befall you, no disaster will come near your tent. So, don't worry, fear not although it may not seem like it, believe me when I say, there are more with you than are against you and you DO NOT STAND ALONE! I know this seems strange, but I wanted to speak directly to you. Let my words uplift and encourage you. I have been there, loving my haters even when I have been wronged. At those times I showed love, care, and concern. Loving my haters, when I tried my best to support them and take them through doors God opened for me. I did everything within my power to make them shine. And in return was I disappointed. Yes, I was hurt, and devastation came for me, the pain was so deep that I could barley breathe as if the very life was being stripped from me. It was then that God reached down from heaven and touched me with his loving arms. In those times, I was comforted by the angles of God. In those times I heard a still voice say RISE UP from the ashes you rise, shake the dust, and move forward. I knew it was God speaking to me, yes me with the broken heart and wounded spirit. My insides began to come together, and my tears began to dry. I was breathing a little easier now and I could open my eyes. I felt the room fill with oxygen and I was able to take a deep breath in and as I exhaled, I felt the presence of God in the room. I asked, "Why, God did I have to experience that kind of pain, the hurt was overwhelming, and I felt I was so alone?" The voice said, "I commanded you to love them, I NEVER told you to give them your HEART." That answer shook me to my core, with everything breath I cried out to God and responded, "Lord, please forgive me." He said it again, "I never told you to give them your Heart, which is reserved for me." In that moment I received the revelation of what God meant and what it meant for me. This was a turning point for me that would change the game and the trajectory of my life forever. See, I have always been a lover of people. Being one that loves hard and forgives quickly. I try never to hold a grudge or issue against people for long periods of time. I have found holding onto issues in relationships only makes matters more complicated. I have often found myself apologizing first to keep the peace. I learned early to apologize quickly and move on beyond what was happening. I get it now, and I hope this is helping you because in that moment what I found out is that I was loving people all wrong and not at all because I was giving them what was reserved for my heavenly father, my heart and it was not meant to be. God began to reveal to me, man looks on the outward appearance, but he looks on the heart." It is not the height, strength, stature or resume God was looking for. Instead, as the Apostle Paul stated in Acts 13:22, God said, "I have found in David the son of Jesse a man after my heart, who will do all my will." And there is it ladies and gentlemen. We are to guard our hearts. That does not mean put up barriers or walls. No, it means to love people for who they are and right where they are. You never have to be a door mat for anyone, not mother, father, daughter, son, neighbor, or friend.

"Remember, that the happiest people are not those people getting more; but those giving more." *H. Jackson Brown, Jr.* Never stop being you, that is what the enemy our adversary wants. Know the enemy is the enemy. Your mother, father, sister, brother, neighbor, and friends they are NOT the enemy.

You must first love God, love yourself and then love others. To thine own self be true then and only then will the wrong people not matter because you are covered. Our heavenly father loves us beyond our faults. I know I have grieved God and done things in this life that was not pleasing to him and for that I have asked forgiveness. I know I have hurt people at some point. I try to ask for forgiveness when I realize it. Have you asked forgiveness of those you have wronged? If not, you might want to consider doing that right away because forgiveness frees you. **There isn't anything that we have done, should have done, or that has been done to us that can keep God from loving us.** His love is constant and unstoppable. Know that the Lord is with you today and loves you beyond measure! *Romans 8:38*

Many are called but few are chosen, if you are reading this,

I believe you are chosen. Leaders on the front who pour out daily always giving of yourselves. King Solomon said it best: "Above all else, guard your heart, for it is the wellspring of life." *Proverbs 4:23*

I encourage you to guard your hearts. There is a time of refreshing, renewing, and refilling that you must be sure to allow yourself to experience otherwise you will burnout.

Three reasons why we must guard our heart.

1. Our heart is valuable, it is where our dreams, desires, and passions dwell. It is the core of who we are. We should make guarding our heart a top priority.

2. It is the source of all that you do. Our heart overflows into who we are and what we do, the decisions we make, and the actions we take. The heart is the second most important organ in our entire body. It is where the blood flows. When something goes wrong with heart, everything else is at risk. If the heart is unhealthy, it has an impact on everything else. Your family, your friends, your ministry and even your legacy. It is important to guard your heart. I understand better now why God does not allow man to see our hearts.

3. It is constantly under attack: We need to know that there is an enemy that is determined to see us be destroyed and will stop at nothing to make sure that happens. Remember, who the enemy is, he uses all kinds of weapons to attack our heart. For me, these attacks come in the form of situations and circumstances that involve those I love most. Also, the things I am passionate about like my family, friends, ministry, and career. The enemy comes to disappoint or discourage me and tries to cause me to get frustrated, quit, and throw in the

towel. We must not allow that to happen. I say to you guard your heart, give your heart to God, and allow him to protect It. He created it and knows what is in it.

People will always fail us, but it is up to us to not expect more of someone than they can give. Love them for who they are and where they are. "If you judge people, you have no time to love them." *Mother Teresa*

Finally, love yourself because if you do not love yourself, you cannot love others. Man looks on the outer appearance, but God sees the heart. Now I only in part; then I will know full, even as I have been full known. And now faith, hope and love abide, these three; and the greatest of these is love. *I Corinthians 13:13*

You are fearfully and wonderfully made, there is greatness in you, and you are here to do great things. Never give up on your dreams. "Every great dream begins with a dreamer. Always remember, you have within the strength, the patience, and the passion to reach for the stars, to change the world." *Harriet Tubman*

Never, stop loving or doing good in this world. You must be the change you wish to see in the world. *Mahatma Gandhi*

We Live In A World...

We live in a world full of love hate and pain,

so what do we do when out comes the rain,

we search and we pass through the walls and the gates,

we look for the love to overcome the hate,

no pain, no gain is what they say,

but when the sun comes out, we know we made it
to another day

we live in a world, yes we do,

but the world does not have to live in us,

not me or you.

Dr. Nephetina L. Serrano

Joan Wakeland

Don't drink the poison!

by Joan Wakeland

Life is a journey, and every journey has good days and bad days. You will walk, run or ride on paved roads and unpaved roads. Along life's path you will see the good, the bad and the ugly.

You are not promised a rose garden, and even if you were, you would be tempted to smell the roses or cut them. Roses are so beautiful! You have to know how to deal with the thorns though, if you really want the roses. You take your time when you are going to remove them from the branch, you circumvent the thorns. You are very patient. Why? You don't want the petals to fall off, you don't want prickles in your hands! You only want a beautiful rose with a nice smell!

I would like to share with you three negative experiences, trust me there are more. These experiences impacted me. Sometimes obstacles and negativity can be a gift that shifts you to your greater heights! These experiences allowed me to be a stronger person. They allowed me to have more confidence and self-worth. I have forgiven the perpetrators because I cannot ask my Lord and Savior to forgive me if I cannot forgive people who did me wrong! Today, I know how to negotiate better, how to build better relationships and how to prioritize! I know not to sweat the small stuff; I know how to stay focused shutting out distractions that will deter me from achieving my goals!

I chose three-time frames in my life because the thorns, the obstacles, the challenges and naysayers are there for the young and the old. Negative experiences are not going to pass you by. It is how you react to them that will give you the peace, happiness and joy that we all deserve. I have been transparent, because writing this is so cathartic for my soul! I am hoping that my experience will allow you to realize you are not alone in this wonderful journey! It is up to you to make good choices, don't be a doormat for anyone! Stand up for yourself!

Pamper yourself! Love yourself and know your true self-worth!

Incidents that happen to you between 2 years old and 12 years old make a lasting impression! It is the formative years where everything positive should be encouraged to happen. We are emotionally shaped during this stage of our lives.

When I was 9 years old, a teacher took her bitterness out on me. All the children were standing for roll call. We were back from recess, and she always checked us in upon our arrival. We were listening to her ranting about the children not getting back from recess on time. While we were out of the classroom, she was actually quarreling with another teacher. I was the first to return to the room, so I overheard them. She was a very unhappy individual. Unfortunately for me, a boy that was standing behind me chose to be puckish. He was untying the bow at the back of my dress. I turned my head to see who was touching me.

What happened next was painful for me. I felt her wrath as she whirled her leather belt over my back. I thought she was going to hit the boy who cause the trouble. Oh no, it was me that caused her grief. She told me that I should go and live in a glass house if I did not want to be touched! One would think she would hit the boy who was distracting me. She took an adult problem to the schoolroom. Shortly after my parents moved me from that school. They knew what was happening. She had issues with my father and mother. This was her opportunity to unleash her anger! I came in early from recess and knew that she was quarreling with another teacher so that was another impulsive reason to hit me. I now knew too much. Today, I am happy to know that beating on children is not allowed in the school room.

When I became older, I realized that this individual had mental issues. She enjoyed torturing children. I later learned that she had a girl kneel on a grater. Yes, it is unbelievable that one in the capacity of a teacher would let a child kneel on a metal grater knowing that the spikes would cut into the knees of that child. That was her idea of punishment, Crazy! I forgave her, she was a sick woman.

This experience however allowed me to always listen to my child's day at school. I encourage parents to ask their children "how was your day today? Tell me what happened. Don't accept one or two words, let them talk. Look also at their body language! Look in their eyes, which is the window of our souls. What do you see? Is it joy, tears, fear, excitement or frustration? You should be your child's advocate. You are your child's voice, so what you learn from the daily interactive sessions over dinner will help you to help them!

The second experience was between ages 20 through 24 when I was dating. I met nice guys and I met Jokers! At this age, I was still very naive.

Really Joan? Yes, I grew up overly protected. You would think I lived in a monastery!

I had to forgive my Cheating Boyfriend! He was a Classy Guy. He did all the right things to impress my parents. He would visit and leave at an appropriate time. He would bring me home on time when we went on a date! My parents loved him. He was a

Gentleman. Mr. Classy would bring flowers for my mother. This guy knew how to play her fiddle! I decided to do some research on him after getting phone calls from a female. I learned that I was being courted by a Cheater! He was playing the field with two other girls! Not one, but two! I was hurt, you would be too! I would not be able to continue in that relationship! It is good to know your self-worth. It is not worth compromising! It took a short time to forgive him because I had my mother's support. She encouraged me to release any resentment I had towards "Mr. Classy ". Another one will come by she said, "If you miss one bus, another one will show up in a couple of minutes!" She was right! I started dating another person who became my husband.

Interestingly, I found out that when "Mr. Classy" heard that I was married he was surprised. "When did it happen? "! He asked my girlfriend. He wanted to know if I was dating someone else when he was dating me. Wow, why would that bother him? Ha! Ha! He could cheat on me, but the reverse was not acceptable.

Experience number two may be happening to you right now! Maybe you have had a Prince Charming in shining armor who wooed you only to find out that he was a knave with an oily tongue! Charismatic Cheaters are out there. You may hear from them morning, noon and night. You think this guy really cares for you. When my friend cheated the night before, he would bring me flowers the next time he visited me. Girls love flowers!

Charismatic Cheaters have the ability to cause hearts to break, and at times separate true friendships which can often create emotional baggage in many instances!

When you do the research on the Charismatic Cheater can you face the reality or stay in the stupor of denial? Why can't you believe it? Your girlfriend told you that you may be dealing with a smooth operator! You madly tell her no, but people on the outside looking in see more than you see or choose to see!

Are you carrying emotional baggage?

Why pay the price for what you cannot use! Drop the baggage before you experience hurt! Love yourself first! A deserving person is waiting for you!

"Forgive them Father, they do not know what they do" Jesus forgave them, that is our biblical guide! Forgive the people who hurt you! Don't carry the ton of bricks. Drop it! Forgiveness is the key to happiness!

Why not accept the facts and move on? Don't wish bad things to happen to this individual. If you do, you are the one that's going to hurt. Are you drinking the poison and expecting the other person dead? Lesson here is "Don't Drink the Poison, Let it go!"

Choose to live a life of happiness and not dwell on the mole hills of your journey! Choose a different path when you meet the naysayers, the people who don't have your vision, the people who don't expect too much from you! Choose to spend your valuable time seeking peace, your happiness and your love. Follow your passion, asking for discernment and guidance!

My other experience happened over the age of 50 while I was in the corporate arena.

This experience moved me. I was doing the job that I loved, my clients were happy with me. My dedication to the job left me with little personal time. My weekly routine was work on the job, work at home, then take care of an elderly parent when she needed help.

I went to church on Sundays. I looked forward to Sundays, it was the time to relax although I would sleep if the sermon was boring. That was due to exhaustion.

My manager at the time set the expectations. Everyone had to perform because the company could not afford to pay for underperforming. So, I worked not only my tail off but my hands.

What happened here was so upsetting to me. I was a high achiever and my territory got changed. I spent time, knowing my products and also my competitors. I gave good customer service, and this jolted my being to its core. I inherited an underperforming area which I was to get up to par. If I did not get the numbers up, then I would be out the door!

My clients were not happy with the person who replaced me and three months later I retrieved my old territory. They complained, they would switch using the company products to other alternatives. The company listened!

I believe that you should give a fair day's work for a fair day's pay. I am now happily retired! I have forgiven the people who tried to suppress me.

I gave the three examples in different stages of my life because negativity, hatred, disappointments, and obstacles will always happen. How I reacted to the situation allowed me to be who I am today. I encourage you to consider the source of negativity as a distraction to your real happiness. Stay focused on your path for your freedom, your happiness, your peace and above all things, be true to yourself! Love one another unconditionally. When you serve, you will be amazed at the blessings that will come your way. People that you don't know will be there to help you when you need it! These are the Angels without wings, you are never alone!

HE is with you; HE is the unseen force fighting your Goliaths for you!
I have struggled, but I have not pitied myself.
I have been told that I would not be able to pass my English test by my teacher, I did not listen!
I am a kind woman, don't think I am stupid, I set boundaries! I am paid when you say, "Thank you."
I am paid when you Smile.
I am a forgiving woman who believes her sins are forgiven by the shedding of the blood of Jesus at the Cross!
I have been blessed with peace, happiness, and joy.
I am loved and you are too!

Join me for a free 30-minute consultation and enjoy my online seminar:

joanewakeland@gmail.com

Self-Love & Self Worth are like a Horse & Carriage!
What will Participants take away?
How to walk away without animosity from people who do not serve your purpose.
How to react to stinging criticisms.
What are some strategies for self-preservation?
How to value your time.
How to understand the importance of self-worth.

Violet Williams

Finding myself from the love that was within me.

by Violet Williams

As the youngest of eight and my dad's only daughter, my mother made sure that I knew that when I was born, he was so excited to finally have a little girl. All I can remember from those moments of appreciation is knowing that I was the center of my dad's world. My dad had a whistle specifically for me growing up that he called "a special whistle," that he would use very frequently to call me by my name. However, he is the one named, Violet. My first name was so special to him because it was the name of his niece that he loved very dearly. My mother shared with me that she did not want that to be my name and that she would call me by my middle name Mary-Ann. which everyone else followed. When I was little, I remember waking up to the smell of supper being made in the morning. Before I went to school, my dad would always say you have to have a warm meal to eat before going to school to hold you for the day.

When I was around eight or nine, my parents separated but my dad would always make the effort to come by to take me on a special outing with him. I remember the walks to the neighborhood and when he couldn't come to share a day with me, he made sure I had all the things I needed. I went to my grandmother's house where she gave me clothes to make sure that I had a winter coat during the winter season. There are many more special memories I remember of my dad. The most painful time was when my mother decided to move to California after their divorce and in that moment, I thought about special days that I wouldn't get to share with him. It felt like my dad slipped away. My heart was broken. All I can remember was the sadness in my heart from being separated from my dad, the person that loved me unconditionally was gone from my life.

For years, I resented my mother for leaving my dad and my dad for not fighting to keep the relationship together. As an adult I understand but as a little girl with my dad being the center of my world, leaving him didn't make sense.

I am sure my parents had no idea that them being together was the safest I felt. Life was not perfect by no means however, as time went by, I knew that I would have to forgive my mother to heal. Deep in my heart I was grateful that I had a dad who showed me love unconditionally. My dad always made me feel special. Whenever I think of my dad, I feel grateful I was blessed with a dad who was so kind and always made my world shine. I'm sure he would say that I was the light that shined. Having that light within me was my home.

When I think back on the day of August 13th, 2008, I was leaving work when I suddenly got into a car crash. In the middle of the accident, I heard Gods voice say, "This is your answer." I had no idea the states that I would go through. I didn't know all the mental, physical, and emotional trauma would be exposed in my soul. I did not know the depth of the hurt, pain, damage, unforgiveness, self-loathing, and despair that I was carrying.

I asked God to heal my brain so that I would do what it is that I am here to do. I knew it at that time and in that moment, I would follow through. I will no longer listen to the voices that will lead me down multiple paths. I'm not feeling fearful this time. I will follow up with the path that I know in my heart that will lead me to my purpose. I decided that I will listen and trust no other voice other than my own. I will have faith. I made the decision to stand alone with the strength of God. After making this commitment, all things began to fall into place on the journey to self-discovery, self-worth, self-confidence, self-love, and self-empowerment. The path will take me down a journey where I will grow to love who I am wholeheartedly while fully embracing myself good, bad, the ugly, and learn to accept my whole being inside and out.

How can I be pleasing to myself and how can I be pleasing with others? Those were some of the questions that I began to ask myself after the accident. Many more questions followed. What is it that I want? How do I want to feel? Do I need to depend on the external world to make me feel okay? Am I enough to live the life that I want to live? I remembered God's voice during the accident replay in my mind, "This is your answer." I know that he will meet all of your needs and you're your hearts desires, He holds answers to infinite and eternal. God's word says that he will guide you and lead you to all truth. He can help you to have peace, joy, happiness, and a positive future.

I needed to know the truth he had for me.

I always thought that I was smart and had a good head on my shoulders but after my accident I felt convoluted which made me doubt my decisions. I felt insecure and I lost my confidence. In the past I could fight through those things but with my TBI (traumatic brain injury) things became difficult. I did have individuals to encourage me through the trauma but somehow, I still needed to get my soul back. God came to give me my life back. I began to live more abundantly and forgiving, which helped pave the path to healing my mind, body, and spirit,

As I began to walk this new path to self-discovery, I began to look at myself with eyes of beauty. I looked for forgiveness, compassion, and to see deeper within myself. I began to fully open up to see the power that I have within to speak from my true self. I am fulfilled from God's internal strength, power, love, and grace. I would learn to let go of the pain of the past, the hurt, shame, guilt, and the thought of feeling that I was not enough. I let go of putting other people's thoughts and opinions of me as I welcome and allow myself to receive grace. These lessons have been life-changing but also impactful for my life. Forgiveness is to let go of the past. God says to renew your mind, I've always believed in the concept, but now I think even more with an abundance mindset. Remember to give yourself grace when making mistakes. Know that you are human, and things do happen. Be kind to yourself and love yourself. Take time to do things that are good for you. You cannot pour from an empty cup. Take the time to fill your cup with Gods love, self-love, and truth. It is daily work. I have embraced forgiveness, freedom, and letting go to be fruitful, bearing the gifts of the spirit: Love, joy, and peace. I know my worth and value.

That light will always be my guide to love from within. My one rule for life is to let my light shine as I live from my best spirit of knowing love will always win.

The following scriptures have been instrumental for my self-development. These are a few scriptures I use to meditate daily with psalms 23, Proverbs 3:5,6, John 14:27,

Psalms 119:11 and Philippians 4:6-7

ACKNOWLEDGMENTS

I want to personally thank each one of the Contributing Authors in Volume 1 of Love your Haters listed below.

Kimberly Anderson, Angeline Benjamin, Dr. Barbara Berg, Elizabeth Mejia Celis, Angela Covany, Verlaine Crawford, Virginia Earl, Nicole Fournier Farrell, Belinda Foster, Stephanie the Shopologist, Raven Hilden, Melissa Kahn, Dr. Cherilyn Lee, Jeannette LeHoullier, Mayra Lewis, Debbie Love. Susie Mierzwik, Dr. Robbie Motter, Lori Raupe, Lisa Ray, Kelly D. Smith, Charmaine Summers, Dr. Nephetina Serrano, Joan Wakeland and Violet Williams.

I would also like to thank all that have been a part of this collaboration and my staff at Havana Book Group for all your time, effort, and passion towards this project and the promotion of it. Thank you, Madison Warren, Angel Toussaint, Marcy Decato, Angeline Benjamin, Debbie Love, Dr. Robbie Motter, Stephanie the Shopologist, Lisa Ray and Gemini Productions.

Power and Control Wheel

Abuse is never deserved. Everyone deserves to feel loved,

respected and appreciated for their authentic self.

CPSIA information can be obtained
at www.ICGtesting.com
Printed in the USA
BVHW011539190722
642494BV00008B/112

9 781735 311784